The LakeShore Project

by

Mark D. Vance

Abenteuer Books
San Diego, California
May, 1998
First Edition

The LakeShore Project

by

Mark D. Vance

PUBLISHED IN THE UNITED STATES OF AMERICA
BY
ABENTEUER BOOKS
A SUBSIDIARY OF BLACK FOREST PRESS
539 TELEGRAPH CANYON ROAD
BOX 521
CHULA VISTA, CA 91910

Cover illustration by
Jan Pearson

Printed in the United States of America
Library of Congress
Cataloging-in-Publication

ISBN: 1-881116-91-3

Prologue

February 1992

A hush fell over the huge dining hall as the lighting dimmed into darkness. A huge green symbol on the front wall provided the only remaining source of light. It formed a sphere of sorts, resembling an atlas, only with a large letter 'G' centered in the middle.

Suddenly, a lone spotlight burst into the darkness, and a cheer rose from the crowd of onlookers when a very well dressed businessman walked across the stage to the podium. His suit was conservative, blue–striped, double –breasted and tailored perfectly to fit his trim frame. He smiled and raised a hand to silence the enthusiastic group. After another minute of applause throughout the large ballroom, the audience began to take their seats again.

"Thank you," the business man said graciously. "Thank you very much for your kindness."

He smiled as the crowd roared again, his bright blue eyes sparkling in the beaming of the spotlight.

"I'm very glad to be here today. I have great news for all Global Computer Solutions stockholders." He paused for a moment until the polite applause subsided, then continued in a raised voice so as to excite the crowd. "Global has just completed another banner year. We have exceeded every. . . yes, every single financial goal set for last year. Global is now, without a doubt, the largest, most successful computer software consulting firm in the nation. And, every person in this room has played an important role in realizing that goal."

On either side of him, board members sat proudly at their private tables, basking in the success of the company, not to mention the success of their wallets. . .as they silently added up the bonuses they were about to bestow upon themselves. Their applause was as much for themselves as for Global's good fortunes. All, that is, except for one man sitting on the end, close to the stage exit. He, too, wore the conceited smile, but at the same time, was a bit distracted as he strained to search the room. . .for something.

"From this day forward," the speaker continued, "Global Computer Solutions will be the company by which all others in the industry shall be measured."

Another standing ovation interrupted the speaker's address. The man at the table clapped dutifully while still scanning the room's perimeter. Two guards were posted at each of three visible entrances to the room. A lone guard stood behind the stage peering through the heavy maroon curtains. He directed the others using a hand held radio, but remained out of sight. All was quiet. Nothing abnormal was going on. The crowd's attention was glued to the speaker; no one moved. There were no stragglers around the room, loitering, coming or going, nothing.

The speech continued with the speaker talking of next year's goals, then long range goals for the company. He alluded to the future of the industry, the technological advances, his predictions for the future of computing, in general.

Outside the building, a midsize Chevy four–door was parked in a far corner of the lot. The engine idled quietly, emitting a small flow of steam from the exhaust into the cold winter air. Inside the car, a black man sat behind the wheel, nervously clutching and releasing it repeatedly. His drawn and tired face showed him to be around 40 years of age, when actually he was nearly ten years younger. The last few months had not been kind to Marcus. His body and face had taken mental and physical abuse, enough to age a man an extra decade. It had to end. He was a kind and decent man. All he wanted was to support his family, to bring home a good living and make his wife and two little girls happy. He couldn't stand living like this anymore. He had tried it their way. It was wrong, and every evening when he hugged his children, another knot swelled up in his gut, just to remind him.

Marcus peered between the beads of water on the windshield. A light snow had started falling only an hour ago, the flakes still melting as they struck the ground. The meeting was almost an hour long now. All was quiet. Through the large glass windows at the entrance to the building, the lobby seemed completely empty.

Oh. . .there was a plan, however flimsy, it was still the best thing he could think of. His family was hidden. They didn't know anything about the mess he was in. He asked them to go to the cabin in Wisconsin, on the Dells. They vacationed there occasionally, and he had convinced them that he only wanted a quiet weekend together. It would be a lazy winter weekend, spent in the cozy warmth of their little hideaway. He would be along later in the evening after he finished some company business. If the plan went right, his colleagues would be exposed before they had a chance to harm his family. Once it was in the open, the threats would be useless. It would only compound the trouble they would be in.

Marcus opened his billfold to a family picture stored inside. He wore an olive suit with a flowered silk tie. He was standing. His lovely young wife sat in a chair, her husband's right hand resting on her shoulder. Beside her, two little girls smiled from ear to ear. The six–year old's big brown eyes glistened, while the four–year old looked up at her mother.

Marcus said a quick prayer and put the wallet back in his hip pocket. He cut the engine and stepped from the car into the frigid night. Pulling his suit jacket on, the same suit as in the picture, coincidentally, he started toward the front doors.

The speaker had been at the podium for 45 minutes and was beginning to drag a bit. With his insights and plans now bestowed upon the crowd, it was time to wrap up his segment. Again he graciously thanked the group and promised the utmost for the year to come. Finally, to continue the meeting, he introduced his Chief Financial Officer, who was to bore them to tears with talk of ratios and budgets and such. The speaker took a seat by the man seated at the end of the table. They shook hands, and he returned to his survey of the room, its exits, the guards, etc.

It still looked clear, not a soul in sight. Marcus was only a dozen yards away from the lobby entrance. But, he didn't see the guard off to the side who lurked in the dimmed light of a pay phone area.

"I've got someone approaching the lobby entrance," he whispered into his radio.

The message was directed to the man behind the curtain, the security chief.

"Is it him?" he questioned the lobby guard disgustedly.

"It looks like him," he paused. "Yeah, I'm sure. It's him!"

"Okay," the chief replied. "Stop him there. Under no circumstances is he to make it into the meeting hall. . .Got it?"

"Got it," the guard answered.

"Units 2 and 3," the chief commanded. "To the lobby right away. Detain the subject at all costs."

Four guards acknowledged his orders, two at the main door and two more at one of the side doors.

"And whatever you do, keep things as quiet as possible." The chief emphasized this command. "I'm on my way."

He hooked the radio on his waist and quietly slipped over to the concerned businessman. The chief leaned out from the curtain far enough to whisper the progress to him. Meanwhile, the speaker from before turned his attention to them, only for a moment and then promptly returned it to the podium, with the CFO's bean counter talk. After updating the businessman, the chief proceeded to his rendezvous in the lobby.

Marcus placed his hand on the cold steel and pulled a door open. He was in. The lobby was clear. Fifty yards in front of him waited the double doors into the meeting and his redemption.

A warm breeze rushed past him and into the cold outside as the door lazily shut itself. The lobby was very bright like a huge spotlight shining down, anxious to betray his presence. Marcus began making his way across the huge distance into the spotlight. His shoes echoed off every wall as each step hit the marble flooring.

"Hold it right there!" A voice rang out from nowhere.

Marcus swung his head to the side where he spotted the lobby guard exiting his dark hideout and entering the main lobby. In one hand a night stick twitched daringly. The man was moving just short of a jog, moving to cut Marcus off before he reached those doors.

It was now or never. Marcus broke into a jog, trying to beat the guard. The lobby guard instantly jumped to a full sprint. But that was the least of his problems. The same two doors that he needed so desperately to reach were suddenly anything but where he needed or wanted to be. They swung open, and two more guards came through.

Marcus slid to an abrupt stop, almost falling because of his wet dress shoes. He stopped only a few yards short. As he spun around to face the front door, he caught a glimpse of the other two guards entering the lobby from the opposite side. That made five now. What a mistake this had been, one that he feared may cost him his life.

He did the only thing possible. . .run, and broke into a sprint towards the exit. The guards chased him across the lobby. He may have gotten away, but the lobby guard, who was already running towards him, only had to change his direction a bit to cut Marcus off.

The guard leapt into the air, clothes-lining Marcus across the neck with his right arm. It sent them both to the floor hard. That was all he needed to do as the other four guards converged around the scene.

Marcus tried to jump back to his feet, but another guard snapped his foot across the waist high jaw of their objective. It sent him to the floor again. Two guards grabbed his arms and yanked him to his feet.

"Hold it a second," the lobby guard snapped as he was picking himself off the hard floor.

The two who were restraining Marcus obeyed his request. He slowly walked over to the spot where his night stick had landed and picked it up from the marble. Marcus fidgeted with fear, as he suspected the guard's next action. But it was no use. He couldn't break the hold of the other two.

"Why didn't you stop when I told you to, boy?" the lobby guard spouted challengingly.

Marcus gave no answer. The guard circled him as a vulture high over its prey. Suddenly, he grasp the stick with both hands and swung it, baseball style, into his captive's kidney. The wood thumped hard against Marcus, taking his breath away. He coughed in agony while the guard chuckled.

"I'm sorry, I didn't hear you." The lobby guard dared him again.

"Fuck you!" Marcus accepted his dare and choked out between coughs.

The guard, back in front of him now, jabbed the end of the night stick across the jaw of his victim. Blood sprayed from his mouth.

"What was that?" he challenged again.

Marcus was a strong-willed man. He had never backed down in his life.

"I said. . .Fuck you." He pronounced it slowly and clearly.

"Why you lousy. . ."

The guard drew his weapon back again to strike Marcus's face but a sixth member had joined the group of guards. It was the chief. He grasped the stick on its backswing, stopping it instantly. "What in the hell are you doing?" the chief demanded. His voice was full of anger as he strained to avoid yelling. The lobby guard offered no explanation. The chief yanked the stick from his hand and pushed him aside. He gave no resistance. "I told you to keep it clean," the chief lectured. "That meeting's letting out in minutes. Wouldn't it be great for several hundred people to see you beating this guy."

"He was trying to escape," the lobby guard tried to justify.

"Shut your mouth," the chief commanded, his pointing finger inches away from his guard's face. "Get him around back...and clean up this goddamn blood. Now."

Marcus was dazed from the blows and only semi-conscious. When he regained his senses, he was tied to a plain wooden chair in a large room. No one else was in the room, not even a guard.

There were building supplies all around, as though the room were being remodeled. A pile of tools lay in the corner next to a large hole in the plaster. Mixed in with them lay a small saw on the concrete. Marcus spotted it instantly. He knew he had to reach it. That saw was his only hope. With all his effort, he jerked his weight sideways, scooting the chair a few inches. It made a terrible loud shriek as it slid across the dust covered floor. He did it again, then again. It was working.

But suddenly, the door swung open. No guards entered, only two older gentlemen in suits. They had been in the meeting earlier. The first was the nervous one who had been sitting at the end of the table watching the exits. The other was the speaker who had addressed the stockholders only hours before.

They closed the door behind them. There was a strange calmness in their actions, as if walking into a room with a man bound to a chair might be a normal occurrence. The speaker stayed by the door while the other businessman strolled to the center of the room with Marcus.

"I see you're finally back with us," he commented as he surveyed the pile of tools and the progress Marcus had made from the center towards them. With a disgusted look, he asked, "What are you doing?"

Marcus was silent. He couldn't believe how ruthless these people were.

"Why'd you have to do it, Marcus?" the man questioned. "We let you in. You were going to make more money than you ever thought possible. Wasn't that good enough for you? Why have you turned on us. . .after all we've done for you. . .and your family?"

"You leave my family out of this," Marcus demanded.

"Oh, we will. We have the information now. There's no need to involve more innocent people. That would only complicate things. I can't believe you were going to turn this information over to the stockholders," the businessman said, holding a small computer disk into the air. "Were you just going to rush into the meeting and start yelling? Most of them would think you were crazy anyway. . .or better yet, wouldn't even care. After all, they're getting their dividend checks, and that's all they care about."

"It's wrong. I didn't want anything to do with it." Marcus had to get his feelings out, for whatever good it would do. "I worked hard to get where I am. If I wanted to be a criminal, I could've stayed on the streets, selling drugs or something. But I didn't. I went to college, and I've worked my ass off for you ever since."

"You're nothing," the speaker screamed from beside the door. He walked forward into the light. "We made you what you are. We gave you the break you wanted. And now, this is how you repay us?"

Marcus saw the hatred in his cold blue eyes and knew that this man was insane.

"It doesn't matter now," the speaker continued. "We've got the disk. You're not important to us anymore."

"I wish you had joined us," the businessman remarked despairingly.

"I believe these treasonous actions are unbecoming of a Global employee," the speaker started again. "We gave you every opportunity to excel, Marcus, but you just keep letting us down. I'm afraid your employment is now terminated."

With that statement, the speaker pulled a handgun from under his suit jacket and pointed the barrel into Marcus' chest.

Marcus braced himself for the shot. He thought of his wife, his two little girls growing up without their father. A tear swelled in his eye; he missed them so terribly already.

"No," the other businessman yelled. "We still have lots of people here. Someone might hear the shot."

He grabbed the speaker to keep him from pulling the trigger. The speaker was furious. He wanted to shoot this man himself. He wanted to watch him die.

The speaker finally put the gun away, and the other man released him. As soon as he was free though, the speaker kicked Marcus in the chest, sending the chair to the ground on its side.

With the direction the chair had fallen, Marcus was turned away from them, unable to see what happened next. He was terrified, but at least he was still alive.

The speaker paced the floor. He was unwilling to allow someone else the pleasure of this kill. Finally, he noticed the tools stacked in the corner and excitedly ran to them. Marcus heard the clanking metal as the speaker chose his weapon. He couldn't have imagined what was next.

The businessman watched as his boss pulled a dirty sledgehammer from the pile. His expression was unchanged. After all, this would be much more acceptable. There was no noise to be concerned with, so he just watched intently.

"Okay, where were we?" the speaker asked as he walked towards Marcus.

He bent down from behind so Marcus could just see his face. The icy blue eyes were there again, so tiny and cold.

"I believe I was telling you. . .," he paused for an eternity. "You're fired!"

The speaker raised the sledge way over his head and swung it downward with every ounce of his strength. Marcus never even saw it. The heavy steel end struck Marcus in the forehead and buried itself to the handle. His skull made a cracking thud as it collapsed, spilling blood and other pieces around the chair. The blow killed Marcus instantly. . .widowing his lovely wife and orphaning his children.

Undaunted, the speaker tossed the bloody tool aside and calmly walked over to the door. He tapped on it lightly, and the chief guard entered. When he saw the carnage in the center of the floor, he almost fainted. But he hid it well, not wanting the speaker to view any signs of weakness.

"Clean this shit up," he ordered calmly.

"What do you want me to do with the body?" the guard asked meekly.

"I don't care," the speaker answered uninterested.

"Make it look like an accident," the other businessman joined in. "Put him in his car, drive it somewhere and wreck it. Make sure its a bad one, too."

"Make sure the wreck is somewhere normal, somewhere he would be," the speaker added.

"Yes sir," the chief obeyed.

"I'm going to need a replacement programmer on my staff now," the businessman stated, turning his attention to the speaker.

"Fine, go ahead and find someone," the speaker answered as he headed for the door. "And try to make it someone we can keep in line this time, someone who'll do their job and not be so goddamn nosy."

"Yes sir," the businessman answered. He knew when not to push too hard. "I'll get on it tomorrow."

Chapter One

May 1997

A lone beam of morning sunlight sneaked through the part in the curtains, finding its way to the bed where Zach lay sleeping. A harsh buzzing burst out from the alarm irritating him enough to fulfill its purpose. Zachery Crawford turned to the alarm to hit the snooze button and sneak another 15 minutes of sleep before it rang again. But it was too late. The sunlight caught him square in the eyes as he fumbled with the alarm. He wouldn't be able to fall back to sleep now.

The time was 6:00 A.M. as Zach sat up on the edge of the bed. He walked across the thickly carpeted room to the balcony window, where he opened the drapes to expose a beautiful sunrise on the lake. Squinting harshly, he walked out on the balcony into a stiff cool Lake Michigan breeze. From his balcony, Zach had a fantastic view of the Chicago skyline, as well as the lake. It was a far cry from the farmhouse he had been raised in. After a moment, the windy city breeze bit at Zach, and he walked back into the bedroom to rid himself of the morning chill.

He had been very lucky, having come from a small town and a family without much money. He was a good looking young man with a bright future at a big computer programming corporation. . .and already well on his way. His apartment was a dream, situated in a suburb of Chicago, a 30th floor condominium overlooking Lake Michigan as well as the wonderful skyline of this bustling city. He lived in luxury, a large three–bedroom, two–bath apartment, with a sunken living room and wraparound balcony. The back wall of the living room was completely glass, allowing a marvelous view from anywhere within the room. The floorplan was that of a split bedroom layout, with the huge master on the right and the other two to the left of the spacious living room.

As he splashed water on his face trying to wake up, Zach glanced into the mirror. Peering back at him was a well-conditioned man. He was of only average build, maybe 6'0", 190 pounds, but regular exercise was obvious. His arms bulged slightly with muscles, the biceps large and round and the triceps pushing out with small rippling strands across the back of his arm. His chest expanded from his frame on top and diminished into a thin washboard waist. A deep dark tan covered his entire body accentuating the thin line of dark blonde hair running from his chest down. His hair was a dirty blonde color. He wore it parted on the right, but brushed back the wavy strands. He also wore a thick full mustache, with blue eyes and dark complexion that gave him a ruggedly handsome appeal, a Marlboro man sort of look. Zach was proud of his appearance. He'd worked hard to maintain it with a regular, strict schedule of workouts.

Zach hadn't had a particularly rough childhood, but he didn't grow up with money either. At age 32 now, he had been working since age 15, when he, like many other teenagers, took a fast food job. Later, he had lucked into a part-time job as a computer operator at a small local bank. This was where his first interest in computers had been sparked. While at that job he began to study books and manuals on computers and became more fascinated all the time. This seemed to come natural to him, and without realizing it, it somehow became what we wanted to do with his life. Working at the bank and doing odd jobs here and there, Zach put himself through a rather average state college earning a degree in computer science and graduating near the top of his class. But, after nearly six years working at the bank, he realized it had no further opportunity to offer him.

At the suggestion of his cousin living outside of Chicago, Zach took a vacation to search for a job with a future, one with a big company in a big city. What he found was a position with Global Computer Solutions Corporation based in Chicago, Illinois. Global was one of the largest independent software houses in the country, with customers across the country and abroad. It developed custom information systems for Fortune 500 companies on a regular basis. It had also grown into one of the largest outsourcing houses in the states, doing the computer processing for virtually dozens of huge companies from private industry to banks to government projects.

Over the next five years, Zach had come through the ranks and now managed a large team of programmers. This company had become his life. The work spilled over into evenings and into home life, as the terminal on his desk would seem to concede. But he knew this was the lifestyle he wanted, and the excess work wasn't that big a price. . .was it?

It was early yet, just 7:00, but this was not a concern for Zach, who was not measured in 8 to 5 terms as many other employees. His work schedule had been left alone by superiors, having proven himself so invaluable over the years. He usually arrived at the office by 8:30 to 9:00 in the morning.

After a few miles on the treadmill and a quick shower, Zach relaxed for a bit and read the morning newspaper as he sipped a cup of rich Colombian coffee, a present from a recent client in Bogota. With the coffee finished and Sports and Business sections reviewed, Zach tossed the paper into a corner of the couch that filled the sunken living room and rode down to the building's private garage.

"Good morning, Paul," Zach offered to the watchman.

"Morning Mr. Crawford," a short plump man answered. "You seem very chipper today."

"Yeah. I guess I am. What about you?" Zach's question was genuine. From the moment he moved into the building several years ago, Paul had been nothing but courteous to him. And he prided himself on his judgment of character.

"Pretty good. I hope to get some fishin' in later this afternoon."

Zach continued away, through the garage. Many people in downtown Chicago didn't own cars, or at least tried to avoid driving them often. With traffic and parking, it was more of a nuisance than it was worth. But this was another luxury that Zach afforded himself as he stepped into his dark blue BMW convertible. The morning dew had already burned off, so he lowered the canvas top and slid on a pair of Oakley's.

It was only seven miles to the office, but a 30 minute drive in the bustling city traffic. This was going to be a beautiful day, Zach thought to himself. It was one of those bright blue spring days when everything seems fresh and clean, yes, even in the windy city. There was a special air of confidence around Zachery this morning, though. He was always a confident young man, but this morning was different. His attitude was better than normal. He had just wrapped up a very important project and was due for the post-project meeting with his boss this morning. These meetings were almost always pleasant and rewarding. Even as seasoned as he was, Zach was still bubbling with anticipation.

He turned from the freeway into the traffic and negotiated the last few corners before arriving at the office. Global had its corporate headquarters here at the northern outskirts of the city. The grounds covered approximately ten acres of prime commercial property overlooking Kennedy Expressway, one of the many freeways feeding people into this bustling city. The compound was landscaped beautifully, with varying greenery and a small pond to the left of the parking area.

In the middle of the grounds was the Global corporate headquarters building. It was a modern seven–story building with sharp pointed corners instead of an ordinary square structure. The outside of the building was covered in a bronze colored glass.

As Zach entered the drive, he slowed to approach the main center gate. The entire grounds were surrounded by an eight-foot high barbed wire fence with gates at either side and this main gate in the center. A guard stepped from a small guard house at the gate and checked him before continuing. When the man saw who it was, he just moved aside and motioned Mr. Crawford through.

Zach waved at the man as he passed through the fencing, then drove on toward the building where a private parking spot awaited him close to the entrance. He pulled in, hopped out of the car and made his way toward the entrance. Zach looked up the side of the building, the sun reflecting brightly off bronzed glass. He grinned again. What a beautiful day!

The bottom floor served as a reception area and public relations more than anything. Plants and trees scattered the lobby like a greenhouse.

Zach stepped through the large entrance into the building lobby, which was already crowded with customers and company representatives waiting or discussing business with each other. He made his way to the left side where he stepped into a corridor containing several elevators. After a moment, one of the doors slid open, and Zach walked into the elevator pressing the button marked "6." The elevator was silent as Zach watched the illumination displaying each floor it passed.

Above the lobby, the next several floors included the majority of the offices and personnel doing the everyday accounting and sales. These floors were wide open areas with tall partitions, but no walls. People ran about their daily tasks between the small corridors created by the partitions, like mice through a maze.

They stopped on four and picked an older woman up. She rode to the fifth floor, which housed all normal computer personnel and their offices. Zach didn't recognize her even though this was his floor and figured that she worked on a different team. All the professionals such as Zachery were housed here. But today he passed his office by on the way to six.

The sixth floor had a few select offices but was mostly consumed by million dollar computer equipment. These offices belonged to the top information systems people. Since data processing was Global's business, these were many of the top managers within the company. As Zach exited, one person remained on the elevator. The COO, Chief Operations Officer, rode the final flight to the top floor, which was reserved for only senior executive management. The president, vice president and a few seldom used offices of little known board members were the only rooms up there, in what many jokingly coined the ivory tower. A massive boardroom which few were ever privileged enough to see was the only other thing Zach knew of up there. The company was run from that floor, all the key decisions taking place right there. It was a strictly run business, and this seemed to work, judging from the company's annual reports over the last decade, not to mention the lifestyle of the company's management.

On the sixth floor, a small lobby was just outside the elevator with several chairs and a table. Across the room from the elevator, a set of large steel doors with a small window marked the entrance to the computer room. A camera from the sophisticated security system surveyed the hall as he approached the door. Zach glanced at it. Global had kept the security tight up here since before he had started some four years ago. This was no surprise to him, however; most of the programming and processing done here was very sensitive. At any given time, Global may be developing software ranging from general accounting applications, to banking programs, to government projects. And besides development, millions, maybe billions of dollars worth of information flowed through here in the outsourcing work being done. Global had to maintain tight security to satisfy its customers, or it would quickly be out of business.

Zach reached to the right of the doors where there was a small panel. He typed in a short sequence of numbers, waited a moment for the latch to click, pushed the door open and walked in. A white tile floor angled upward to another couple of doors leading directly into the main computer room. No windows revealed the room on the other side.

Zach stepped through the doorway, where he was greeted by a colleague. It was one of the men who worked on his programming team. The man was slightly older than Zach and a little chubby. He had worked for Zach for nearly a year now, and while he was a decent programmer, there just wasn't any drive. They had roughly the same seniority, but Zach had always been promoted first, and over time, had risen to a management position over the gentleman. He seemed content at mediocrity, never asserting himself, which drove Zach crazy. The man wore a short beard and kept his dark hair combed over the top in an attempt to cover a balding head.

"Good morning, Zach," the man said, walking over to him. "Looks like it's going to be a nice day out, huh."

"Yeah, it's already warming up, Roger," Zach answered. "How're things running today?"

"Fine so far."

"Good. Is John here yet?" asked Zach.

"Yeah, Zach, he's in his office."

Zachery looked across the room to a door on the other side, which led to the office. Then he scanned the computer room. It looked like something from a science fiction movie. The main room measured 70' X 50'. It was purposely placed on the sixth floor where it would be close to the air conditioning units located on the roof of the building. And, it used to be that when old equipment was replaced, it was easier to have it landed on the roof by helicopter and brought down through a special freight elevator. But today's computers continued to get smaller and smaller, and that didn't really matter anymore.

The entire floor of this room was constructed of the same brilliant white tile as in the hall. A small room to the left housed six uninterruptable power supplies, commonly called UPS's. These boxes fed the system its power, and in case of a power failure, they could run the system for nearly an hour, more than enough time to wait for repairs or shut the system down in an orderly fashion.

The main room contained all other major equipment. To the left, racks lined the wall with virtually thousands of wires protruding from the backs of routers, csu/dsu's, patch panels, etc. Huge masses of information flowed through these little black boxes, through the fiber optic backbone, through the T1 lines serving the field. Global spent a great deal of money every year staying current on technology.

Several walkways were created across the room by the placement of the rest of the hardware. A row of disk drives housing hundreds of gigabytes of data, ran up the left side. Thousands of programs and data files developed by Global lived right here on these disk storage units. Various lights flashed intermittently on the disks and input/output routers, indicating use from somewhere on the vast system.

Toward the middle of the room was a bank of processors, effectively acting as the heart of the system. In the sixties or seventies, one or two units would have run the show, but in today's world of distributed processing and open systems, the behemoths of yesteryear had given way to smaller multi-vendor, multi-processor configurations. Machines from all the major players lined up against each other, from IBM, HP and DEC UNIX boxes to NT offerings from vendors like Dell and Compaq. A low undertone of noise filled the room from the dozens of tiny little cooling fans whizzing away. Against the far right side, several printers pounded away, killing more trees than any conscientious human being cared to ponder.

The computer room was also monitored by several surveillance cameras placed in the corners. Most of Zach's men thought these were just for looks. Even Zach wasn't sure; the explanation for them was that they were to monitor the computer room, just as a part of the security procedures. None of the operators bought the story, though. The cameras were just there to impress clients when tours of the facility were given.

Hundreds of lights flashed on the csu/dsu's, disk drives clattered continuously, printers spit paper out at a rate too fast to even read, and the sound of cooling fans rose over it all. This was a multi-million dollar system, and it was at his disposal.

Zach knew and understood this machine better than he knew his best friend. He'd certainly spent countless hours with it, weekends, late nights and holidays. The same couldn't be said for the quantity or quality of time he'd spent with friends in the last five years.

Zach loved the way it felt. He was very good at what he did, and he knew it. He had been approached by countless headhunters, and even occasionally by competitors of Global, all trying to lure him away. But Global had been very good to him, so he'd always returned the favor. He felt a strong loyalty to John and to his company and thoroughly trusted them. And, if it was still possible in this day and age, he fully expected to stay with Global...someday retiring with his cheap gold watch.

He walked past the processors and through the set of double doors on the far side of the room. From this point things were different. The hall was plushly carpeted, lit by a row of small brass light fixtures designed to have an old –fashioned gas lamp look to them. Zach walked to the end of the hall, stopping at the far left–hand door where a small desk and secretary guarded the room.

"Is he in?" Zach asked the lady.

"Yes sir," she nodded. "He's expecting you, Mr. Crawford."

Zach smiled at her and knocked lightly before entering.

"Oh, I've been expecting you, Zach. Come on in and have a seat." The man folded up the newspaper he'd been reading and put it aside as he leaned forward to his desk.

"Good morning, John," Zach said making his way to a high backed leather chair in front of the desk John sat behind.

John was an older man than Zach, around fifty. He was of average height, graying short hair and very fit and trim looking. He had a hard, shrewd look to him, but Zach had never had any problems with him. Since he had been here, it was almost like John had watched over him and led him along like a mentor of sorts. He fully suspected that he might be in line for John's position when he retired, and this was why he had been tutored and helped by John over the years. For now though, John was still his superior. As a matter of fact, he was quite a few people's superior, his of-ficial title being Vice President, Development Services. What this meant was that John was single-handedly in charge of anything and everything that involved the projects that Global did. And since this was a computer software company, that was the majority of the business. Zach had thought of this responsibility before. With only the board members, president and the executive vice president above him on the ladder, John was one of the most powerful men in this billion dollar corporation. Zach's ambitions often led him to thoughts of the future. Yes, one day he would succeed John.

John shifted in his seat before he began. "Well, Zach, what do you have for me?"

"Everything looks great," he answered after drawing a deep breath. "We went live two weeks ago. . .seen very few issues come up. I have a man on site for the rest of this week to keep an eye on things."

"Good," John said nodding his head slightly. "Do you have any details outlined for me yet?"

"Yes, I have a summary report written up in my office, and I believe I copied you on the cutover report to the client. I'll bring it up in a few minutes." Neither of them said anything for a moment, so Zach began to elaborate on his report, thinking that John was waiting for more details. "Mexicana Shipping came in right on the time line. . .actually a few days ahead of schedule. And, as you know, the applications were totally financials, including general ledger, accounts payable and accounts receivable. They've all been in production for almost two weeks now. Like I said a minute ago, Wilson is on site for support purposes and any little problems that might have slipped by us during system testing. Plus, their first month end close is coming up, so he'll be doing a little handholding during that process, too.

I don't have the final dollars yet, but there were a few unexpected expenses. I don't think there's anything bad enough to cut into our margin."

"Well I'm sure there won't be any problems, Zach. . .I just wish all our projects went as smoothly as yours do."

Zach grinned a little at this compliment. Zach wasn't worried about John's lack of words; this was just his nature. John didn't say things out of the blue. If there was nothing to say, he was quiet. He thought everything through very carefully before acting. It was probably one of the reasons for his great success.

"Do they seem to be happy with the system? How's that jackass project manager of theirs?" John leaned back in his chair.

"He's no problem. I figured him out a long time ago. He loves to hear himself bitch, but there's never anything to it. Hell, he calls over here about once a week. . .and I just let him vent while I work on expense reports." Zach chuckled as he continued, "He just has to be stroked a bit here and there, and he's happy. Why, is there a problem?"

"No, no. I was just asking. I remember what a pain he was in the negotiations before the contract was signed."

John stood up and walked over to a large window behind his desk. It afforded a terrific view. He watched the traffic roar by for a moment, then walked around the desk to the side where Zach was sitting. He leaned on the heavy desk, bracing the unsupported half of his body with his left leg still firmly planted on the floor.

Zach was getting a bit concerned. There was something more to this meeting than the usual wrap-up. Maybe he had been wrong about the jackass project manager. He couldn't imagine what the problem might be, or even tell if there was one. This was one attribute Zach just couldn't master about John. John had a hell of a poker face. He could hide what he was thinking, leaving you totally in the dark. Zach tried calming himself, reasoning that nothing was really wrong. Besides, he couldn't let John know he was nervous. But it must have been too late.

"What's wrong, Zach?" John turned his head to one side, not parting his eyes from those of Zach.

"Nothing. Why?"

"You just seem a little uptight."

"No," Zach answered. "It just seems like this isn't really a meeting about my project." Zach was never afraid of being straight with John.

John paused a second before continuing. "Zach, as always, I'm very pleased with your work. This is absolutely nothing negative, so don't worry."

Zach began to relax a little as his curiosity rose, but still wasn't ready to lower his guard.

"Since you've been with Global," he was very slow and deliberate with his words; this was what Zach had learned to expect from John. "Since you have been with Global, you have always done excellent work. I think you've learned and grown with your job, and now you're ready for some more responsibility."

Zach's heart began to race. He had no idea. What did John have in mind for him? Where would he be going from here?

"You know Dave Little, right." John said.

"Yeah, so–so, I guess," Zach acknowledged.

"He's no longer going to be with us. . .and I want you to take over his position."

"What happened to him?"

"We moved him to Europe," John answered quickly. "He is taking a position there. . .just wanted a change of scenery. . ..And as you probably know, we're trying to build a presence in that market. I can't afford to have this position vacant, my boy. I think you're the only one here that can handle it. Oh, you'll have some growing pains, but I'll be available when you need advice. I just don't want to go out of the organization for someone."

There was a long pause. "Well, do you have any thoughts? Are you up to it, Zach?"

"Yes. . .I'd love it." Zach knew he sounded anxious, but John knew him all too well. Why bother playing this 'Let me think it over, I'll have to sleep on it' game?

"Let me fill you in on your new position then." John moved back to the other side of his desk. "Right now you manage the suburban Chicago area project team, and I think this will still be a big part of your job. But now it's a lot more than that. Your new title will be Regional Project Director. This entire region which, by the way, Zach, includes the whole northeast part of the country, will be yours. . .your responsibility. The majority of the job will be decision-making that the men in the field aren't qualified or experienced enough to be making. You know what I'm talking about. The decisions that shouldn't be made by a techie, but by a manager who knows the impact to the bottom line. . .the impact in dollars."

"You'll still be traveling a bit, but it shouldn't be worse than now." John leaned back in his chair watching Zach's reaction. "What do you think so far, Zach?"

"It sounds great, John. How should we handle the transition?"

"You just need to take the ball and run with it, Zach. I can't afford to wait on this one. We can meet weekly if you want. . .or whatever works for you. I'll be here to help you," he answered. "By the way, there are a few fringe benefits also. Effective next week, you will get a ten percent salary increase, and the incentive plan for that position is considerably more lucrative than your current one. Plus, you get Dave's old office here on the sixth floor. It's the one right across the hall."

John was silent for a minute. "That's all I can think of right now, Zach. . .Oh. . .except that your security clearance has been changed to a class A so you have unlimited access to the building and system."

"Thanks, John," Zach said in a shaky voice. "Uh. . .I won't let you down."

"All right, Zach, I'm sure you won't. Now, go check out your new office if you want." John watched Zachery move quickly to the door. "Why don't we have lunch today and play some golf this afternoon? Make a celebration of it."

"That sounds great," Zach said turning back to John. "I'll meet you in the lobby at 12:30."

Zach stepped through the door into the hallway and closed the door behind him. He stood still, John's secretary eyeing him strangely. He had never expected anything like this, his heart pounding and breath short, he was so excited. He didn't know what to think. For that matter he hadn't even known Dave Little was gone. Everything was so sudden. But Zach quickly regained his composure. Suddenly he felt exhilarated rather than faint. Now, except for John, he was top dog. What a great feeling; it was right. There was no doubt in his mind that he could handle the new position and the responsibility it would carry. Another step up the ladder. His career was soaring.

He walked across the hall and put his hand on the brass knob of the door adjacent to John's. The door to his new office opened slowly. Zach didn't think much one way or the other of status possessions, and this office was just that. But on the other hand, you didn't have an office above the fifth floor unless you were somebody. He took a long look around. It was like a small showplace, almost as nice as John's. An entire wall was covered with bookshelves. Like his apartment, the outside wall was glass, with just enough tint to keep the room from being too bright. A private bathroom was located to one side, while the rest of that side of the room included a small wetbar, sofa, coffee table and two chairs to conduct business around. The desk stood centered in the room, and back toward the outside wall to leave a large open space as the room was entered.

It had rounded corners with a light oak finish. The rest of the room's woodwork matched, and behind the desk was a matching credenza. The chairs were of a rich tan leather while the carpeting was light brown.

'*I could get to like this,*' Zach thought to himself. The office was great, more than he could have imagined. Besides the office, he was in a powerful new position and making more money than he ever thought possible. It was quite a leap from working those evening hours processing checks for the bank. And to beat everything, he loved his work. He sincerely enjoyed going to work every morning. What more could a man want? Yes, there were sacrifices, the late hours working at home and on weekends. But he would have time for a personal life later.

After a few minutes savoring his new environment, Zach decided to get down to business. The first thing to do was to get moved into this office. So he went down to his old office. It wasn't bad. At least it was a private office and not a little cubicle like most of the other offices on the floor. Zach looked over the open room of people. They worked feverishly. Phones rang here and there, and the sound of typing rang from every direction. Then it suddenly hit him, these people work for me, all of them.

He sat down at his old desk. It was noticeably smaller, made of pressed wood veneer instead of real oak. Books overflowed a bookcase in the corner, and two small chairs were crammed in, their gray fabric worn and stained. This position was a new opportunity for Zach, and he wasn't going to mess it up. This was going to open a new chapter of his life. He couldn't be happier than he was at this moment.

He began packing and boxing up his belongings to start his new undertaking.

Chapter Two

    John and Zach went to lunch and played golf that afternoon as planned. It had turned out to be a beautiful day as the morning had predicted. The spring colors were in full display, and the afternoon heat hinted at the warm summer days not too far off.

    After nine holes and a drink in the clubhouse, they parted ways, with Zach deciding to make it an early night. . .as something of a reward to himself. He was so excited, though. He couldn't wait for tomorrow to come. . .the sooner the better, so that he could get started in his new position.

    He drove back home in the late afternoon after a losing game of golf. He rarely beat John. After all, John had been golfing on nice afternoons such as this for quite a few years. His tenure at Global was more than 20 years, and for the better part of that time, John had possessed a position that afforded him the liberty to pursue his personal interests, which included golf.

    But Zach was a tremendously improved golfer himself after playing John for several years now. And he was a fierce competitor, one who didn't like to lose, no matter who it was to. He always played to win, no matter what the game. He and John had a good relationship, so the contests on the fairway were never a problem, even when Zach occasionally won. John always gave Zach pointers and tried to look out for him. Once, after a disagreement about clubs, John had purchased a new set of Pings for Zach, to prove he would like them more than his own. John was always looking after him, both professionally and personally.

Zach took it easy that evening. He fixed a small dinner and opened a bottle of wine to congratulate himself. He sat alone at the dining table looking out at the shimmering lights of the skyline. His eyes scanned the apartment. A large pit style couch faced a beautiful stone doublesided fireplace that opened to the other side into the master bedroom. To the right of the fireplace, atrium doors led to the master bedroom. As wonderfully as his life had progressed, the loneliness was still there. It left an uneasy feeling in his stomach as he moved to the living room with nobody to share evenings on the couch or to watch a fire burn on a cold northern night. Quiet evenings like this one brought that loneliness into Zach's conscious thoughts. Would his life have been more complete if he had settled down? There had been occasional girlfriends and lovers, but work always took top priority. They would stick around for several months, but despite all that he had to offer, they always grew weary of taking the back seat in his life. So here he was, still alone. Maybe this was what he wanted. Maybe he was afraid to be close, afraid of commitment.

After dinner, he watched the evening news and part of a movie, but he couldn't stay away from work. The third bedroom of his apartment had been converted to an office. The far wall was lined with bookshelves containing business publications and computer manuals of all sorts. Facing the glass wall was a desk with a notebook computer. This was Zach's private room, his think tank. He devoted many late hours to his career in this room. The room was strictly off limits. No one entered, not friends, lovers, or even the cleaning service. Per Zach's explicit orders this room was not to be disturbed. Unable to resist or fight the boredom, Zach spent the rest of the evening in front of the computer.

He surfed the web, always looking, always learning. Finally, weary eyed, he surrendered to bed several hours later and dropped into a deep sleep almost immediately.

It was late into the morning hours. But now Zach was tossing and turning, not enjoying the peaceful sleep he'd started with earlier. His eyes jerked from side to side under their eyelids. A small bead of sweat rolled across his forehead. Within Zach's mind a story had begun to replay itself from long ago. After being buried deep in the dark corners of his mind for years, it was surfacing once again.

In the dream Zach looked down from above on a group of men around a bright camp fire. They must have been in the woods, somewhere away from any civilization. One of the men was him, younger, but it was definitely Zach! There were eight or ten guys sitting around the fire on a fallen log and on the ground. They were young men, probably about 20 years old. Most wore faded jeans, a varied style of T-shirts. It was quiet all around, but they were all loud, yelling and laughing at each other. One of them threw an empty bottle into the fire, crashing it against a rock. Suddenly, it was obvious that they had all been drinking and were quite drunk. Then one of them said something.

"Are you ready, pussy?" The boy seemed to be the leader of the group. His statement was directed to a guy sitting alone on the other side of the fire. He was the only one of the bunch not drunk. The boy shook his head trying to hide his fear.

"Okay, guys," said the leader. "The wimp says he's ready to go. Zach, you and Jimmy grab him."

The entire group broke into hysterical laughter. They all jumped up grabbing their drinks and stumbling away from the fire. Zach and Jimmy each grabbed an arm of the boy and began to pull him with them. The leader walked over to them and slowly put on a dark jacket with an emblem and three letters across the back. He took a white bandanna from his forehead and used it to blindfold the young man.

"So you want to be one of us. . ... Well, you have to make it through tonight first, boy." The leader yelled to the rest. "Let's go!"

A loud cheer rose from the group as they began walking down a small path away from the light of the still burning fire. Zach and Jimmy brought up the rear pulling the younger sober boy. The boy gave no resistance, however. He wanted to be there.

Then Zach leaned over to the boy and said, "You're in for a night to remember!"

Zach jerked back and forth wildly in his bed. Sweat poured from his forehead down his face. He moaned as the nightmare continued inside his head, finally upsetting him so much that he woke.

He sat up in the bed and wiped his forehead, trying to catch his breath. His mind raced. Why was he having this dream again? Why now? It had been several years since the last instance of the dream. Why did it have to start up again now? With the new position at work, this was the last thing he needed to worry about. He looked at the alarm clock on his nightstand. It was already after five, too late to try to get back to sleep.

Zach got out of bed and got ready for work. He wanted to get there early today. Besides, he needed to change the subject, and his best subject was always work.

When Zach arrived at work, he finished moving into his new office on the sixth floor. Even with everything in it, the new office was literally sparse looking. All of his boxes fit easily in one corner of the room.

That afternoon Zach was still unloading boxes, arranging and rearranging the things on his desk. He sat behind the huge oak desk and propped his feet up on the corner. It felt good. He felt like a big shot. . .Hell, he was a big shot. The phone rang suddenly, breaking the silence. It was John. He wanted Zach in his office; he said it was important.

"John? What do you need?"
"Come in, Zach. . .have a seat."
Zach walked over to John's desk and sat at the same

chair in which he had received his good news the day before.

"Zach," he started, "Do you know about the LakeShore National Bank account?"

"I've heard a little about it. Pre-sales has been over here picking my brain a few times for technical answers." Zach shifted, then imparted more information. "Here's what I know. LakeShore is headquartered here in Chicago with branches throughout northern Illinois. They've been looking for awhile. . .something about vendor troubles, I thought. But, no real promise last I heard."

"We've finally landed the account."

"But I heard that Kansas City outfit underbid us?" Zach questioned, a bit puzzled.

"You seem to know a good bit about this account, Zach."

"I try to stay informed when it's in my territory."

"Anyway," John smiled at his pupil. "They outbid us by almost a quarter million. But, LakeShore likes us. They trust us. . .think we've got the skills to get it done, so we got the nod."

"Why didn't you tell me yesterday?"

"I didn't want to say anything yet, because it was still up in the air. There was a board meeting yesterday, at which time they voted to take our proposal and went ahead and signed the contract. Our people are still working out details in the Statement of Work."

"Can you tell me anything about it?"

"Basically, they're sick of the system they have now and feel like their vendor's been screwing them from day one. They were undersold, and they've been adding equipment since the first month. There've been nothing but problems since they installed it two years ago, and it's time to cut their losses." John shifted in his seat. "They've agreed to invest in all new hardware. That means not only the boxes, but hundreds of workstations, controllers, power supplies, everything; and remember that doesn't include the programming itself."

"What vendor?" Zach jumped in.

"It was between HP and DEC, they went with HP," John responded.

"Well anyway, what's this got to do with me, John?"

"Zach," John paused. "This is going to be a multi-million dollar account for us. With it being here in town, it's very high profile. We're going to be under a microscope by the entire Chicago business community. Lots of visibility."

"I realize that."

"What are your people working on now, Zach?" John chuckled as he asked the loaded question.

Zach could see it now. "We're just wrapping up some things and doing odd jobs. . .mainly updating system documentation. But we're supposed to start on the Smythe Brothers project as soon as delivery is taken on their equipment."

"There's a catch to this LakeShore project, son," John said.

"What's that?" Zach asked.

"They've given us a rather short time limit."

"What?"

"How's six months sound? That's when they want the main system operational. Any custom modifications can be done afterwards."

"How's it sound?" Zach said sarcastically. "Sounds like a damn death march! You mean done. . .in production? John, it usually takes a couple of months just to do a database conversion."

"I know, Zach. You don't have to tell me." John shook his head as though in vain. "But the simple fact is, this is too good a deal to pass up. They're paying top dollar to get it done in a hurry. Evidently the lease is up on the current hardware around that timeframe."

"Do they realize what an undertaking that is? That would put tremendous scheduling demands on us and them. Do they know how much of a commitment that is?"

"The LakeShore management and board assure us of complete cooperation. They want it done. They're committed to the project."

"That's not much time, John. . .not much time at all!"

"We can modify existing banking programs, can't we?" John had done his homework before calling Zach in on this one. But then, John always did his homework. "The ones we developed last spring should provide a good base to start from. . .the ones down in Indiana."

"Yeah, I know the ones. They should work okay I

"Yeah, I know the ones. They should work okay I guess, but they were for a different hardware platform and a different state, which mean possible regulatory differences. Plus, I'm sure there's procedural differences from bank to bank that we'll have to deal with, too," Zach responded.

"Zach, I want your team on the LakeShore project. I can get another team on whatever you were working on." John's voice was strong and convincing. "I need someone on this that I can count on, someone who will do what it takes to keep the project on schedule. . .You are that person. . .I know you'll work over and weekends or whatever you need to do to get it done." There was a short silence. "Well, Zach, can I count on you?"

"I'll need a free hand, no red tape or internal politics. That crap'll kill us."

"Fine, you got it. Besides, you're the boss, my boy, re-member? You make the rules." John walked around the desk to face Zach. "Well, son. . .Can I count on you?"

"Of course you can, John. You know that." Zach an-swered without hesitation.

"This will look awfully good on your record if you get this done on time for us, Zach."

"Yeah, yeah. When will their HP be installed anyway?"

"Our suppliers have promised us that they can deliver within two weeks of when we give the word," John said.

"Give the word."

"I knew you wouldn't let me down, Zach. I took the liberty of setting up a meeting for you with the LakeShore management so you can go over some details." John walked Zach to the door. "Three o'clock this afternoon. I'll email you a document. . .has all the main players, their po-sitions, email addresses, so forth. Do you have time this morning to get familiar with it?" John asked as he turned the doorknob.

"Sure," Zach answered. "I'll wait 'til later to unpack my stuff."

"Zach, with your new job, you might want to hire an extra hand. I don't think you're going to have as much time as you used to."

"Yeah. . .It already crossed my mind. . .I was planning to call up Human Resources this week anyway. Maybe they can get started screening people."

Back in his office, Zach had a chance to think about this. He always welcomed a challenge, even when the odds were so against him. He knew it would be hard, but he also knew he could get the job done. No time like the present to get started. He called an order in to the deli down the road and opened up the email from John. Zach always made sure he was prepared.

That evening Zach sat on the balcony, sipping a 7&7, and pondering the afternoon meeting. It had gone okay. They were very cooperative so far, as promised.

This was a big deal, the biggest project Zach had ever worked on. He was in charge of a multi-million dollar account. There was no time to lose. He'd have to get his team working on it tomorrow. They could at least do some setup, get a project environment established.

HR had left a voice mail late in the day also. They were sending some people over in the morning. What, do they have these people waiting in a cage? Zach hated interviewing people. It was one of the few things about work that bothered him.

Sleep was difficult again that night. He told himself that is was work, but he knew the truth. He didn't want to admit it, but it was the dream. That was the real reason he wasn't asleep. He was afraid to have the dream again. This was the only thing Zach felt he couldn't control, that he didn't have a handle on. He was scared to death of this terrible memory. Instead, he dabbled around the apartment half the night, unable to sleep, until finally his exhausted body collapsed across the sofa.

The next morning Zach paid for his insomnia, waking late and generally feeling blah. What a great day to start a new project. With a crook in his neck and a pounding headache, Zach trudged his way to work as he dreaded dealing with the new hire candidates.

The interviews started mid-morning, with the first candidate waiting in the lobby when Zach arrived. He'd hoped it would be easier than the last time, when it had taken three days and about a dozen people worth of interviews before he found someone suitable.

After a whole morning of interviews Zach was beginning to worry that he was going to break his old record of three days. He had seen six people already. How did these people get past the screening process anyway? Zach had to fight not to show his disgust openly to the interviewees.

The first guy was just out of the service. He looked and acted 100 percent military. While he had computer experience, it was on outdated equipment. Besides, his personality left much to be desired. In fact, plain and simple, he was a prick.

The next applicant was an Asian woman. Her resume was impressive at first glance, but then Zach realized it was all fluff. The more they talked the more something bothered him. Then it hit him. He could barely understand her. It wasn't a prejudiced thought; he just couldn't communicate with her. He wondered if she could be put in front of a client and decided to pass on her for now.

The second and third men just didn't seem to be the type for the job, no real dedication to their work. They had quit or been fired from more places in the last year than Zach had ever worked, total!

And the last two had been to college and seemed okay but didn't have any practical experience. They were completely green. Zach was afraid he was going to have to settle for one of these two. There was nothing wrong with this, but he couldn't afford to dedicate a productive resource to showing someone the ropes when this project was on such a tight schedule. Normally, he would prefer to give one of them a chance. . .so that they could prove themselves, but not this time. There was too much riding on the LakeShore Bank project.

Zach poured himself a glass of water from a pitcher on the oak bookshelves that lined his new office, walked back and sat down behind his desk.

The door opened, and Zach looked up wearily to greet the next candidate. In walked a young woman. Zach was surprised but stood immediately to greet her. She was beautiful. He couldn't take his eyes off her. She walked over to his desk and offered a hand. He shook it gently. It was soft and warm. Zach motioned to a chair where she sat and crossed her legs, exposing most of her thigh to Zach as a slit in her skirt fell open. He looked at her body from top to bottom for a moment, then caught himself. In today's day and age, he had just sexually harassed her.

She sat tall and confident in the high backed chair. Long blonde hair with loose curls draped over her right shoulder and she had big bright blue eyes surrounded by thick dark lashes. His eyes moved downward away from her face. Her neck and chest were richly tanned. She wore a pale pink blouse unbuttoned just far enough to expose cleavage, the satiny material clinging tightly against her breasts. Her hips curved into soft tanned legs partially covered by a navy skirt, covered that is except for that same slit he had noticed a moment ago. Zach moved his eyes down and off of her before she noticed his staring.

"Hi, I'm Taylor Williams." She spoke with confidence and smiled wonderfully at Zach.

"My name is Zachery Crawford. . .Please call me Zach." He smiled at her and opened a folder she had put on his desk. It was quite impressive! She had a fair amount of experience. After a moment he continued. "I see here you have a bachelor's in computer science."

"Yes, I went to school in California, UCLA. . .but I'm originally from just north of here, in Wisconsin."

Zach continued to look through her resume. She had had some experience with the type of equipment they would be using in the bank project. He looked up at her, examining in a different light. She didn't look old enough to be in such a position to have that experience. The skepticism must have shown as his eyes moved back to the folder.

"I have experience, if you'll look at my resume." She wasn't hesitant to speak, like so many he interviewed. Taylor seemed confident in her abilities, and everything about her conveyed it.

"I see that. Why are you leaving your current job?"

"I don't feel like there's any room for advancement," she began. "We aren't a very large company. I basically run the computer operations, but there's only one night operator under me. I just don't see the computer department growing that much in the near future. Five years from now, I'll still be in the same position with the same night operator under me. I can't be happy with that. I really want to make more of an impact on a company."

"Why do you want to work for Global?" Zach questioned. "Or are you just looking for a position wherever?"

"Oh no, I haven't been looking actively. I'm very happy where I am now. It's just that I know that I'm capable of so much more."

"So you're familiar with us. . .I mean Global?"

"Yes. I know that Global is one of the premier software houses in the country. When I heard about an opening, I knew this was an opportunity I couldn't pass up."

Ms. Williams had certainly done some homework before this interview.

"Do you think you've got what it takes to excel here?" Zach held his hand to indicate there was more on his mind. "What I mean is that. . .it's not the same here as in a small company. Some people think it's easier to disappear in the masses, but others are looking for the. . .um. . .dynamics that a larger company sometimes has to offer. Does that make sense?"

Taylor paused for just a moment. She didn't want to sound too egotistical, but she was confident in her abilities.

"I think it does. To me, you have so many more opportunities to experience things. . .different situations, different personalities. I think that's at least a big part in how a person grows. And yes, I do have what it takes," she answered proudly. "Absolutely."

Zach was impressed with her assertiveness.

"What I have available is a medium level programming position. It's not your rookie 80/80 list stuff, but, by the same token, most of it's rather simple programming, at least to start out with. And by simple, I mean file maintenance programs, reporting programs and so forth. . .Uh. . .Do you have any problems with that?"

"No that would be fine. . .to start out with." There was some hint of distaste. "I'm looking to build a career though, not just put in my hours. I would hope that I'd have the opportunity to show what I can do and then be rewarded appropriately."

"Good." Zach closed the folder. "And there is room for advancement here. If your work is superior, it gets noticed. We like to promote from within, so you're always in line when positions open up; and in a company this size, they do open up. Take me for instance, I was just a junior programmer five years ago when I came to Global." Zach changed the subject back to the interview. "Are you willing to work late. . .weekends?"

"Sure, I'm used to working late. With my current job, I get called in probably once a week or so to help the night operator and things like that."

They talked business back and forth for a few more minutes. Zach threw in questions designed to query the knowledge that her resume indicated. She didn't falter once, but he was finding it difficult to concentrate on the interview. His mind was blank. Since asking some general questions, Zach was having trouble moving things along.

"Do you have any hobbies? What do you do with your free time?" Zach finally asked, already knowing that it was inappropriate.

"I usually don't have much free time," she answered, "but I love sports. I exercise to stay in shape and work off stress. I also like softball, tennis, skiing; I guess most outdoor type sports."

"What about golf?" he jumped in.

"Golf bores me, Mr. Crawford," she answered candidly. "I've tried it. I just can't get into it."

Zach's eyes scanned her legs again. She was not lying when it came to staying fit. Her thighs had lean lines of muscular definition, and her calves were nicely rounded. He resisted the temptation to flirt by commenting on her body, even though the perfect opening had presented itself with her answer to the question. Suddenly it dawned on him that she was him; she was a female version of Zach Crawford. She was young, aggressive, and cared about her appearance. More than this, she was smart and knowledgeable.

"I like that. So many people don't take care of themselves these days. And it seems so important in this business. After all, there's not much aerobic value in typing, but the stress sure is there. It's nice to have an outlet to relieve some of it." Zach trailed off, noticing that he might be starting to ramble.

He wanted to ask Taylor more questions but couldn't think of any. And he certainly shouldn't be asking any more personal questions, that is, unless he wanted their next meeting to be in a courtroom.

"Do you have any questions for me?" he asked. Zach always liked to offer this chance to any candidate he interviewed. The prepared candidate always had a few.

"Yes I do, Mr. Crawford," Taylor quickly responded.

"Please. . .Zach," he interrupted.

"Okay, Zach. Do you have a specific project in mind for me or is that still up in the air?"

A classic "power interview" question, Zach thought. And in the interest of not playing along, he decided to answer carefully.

"Well Taylor, I do have a direct plan for whoever it is that I decide to hire."

She was undaunted though. "If you'd care to share some of those plans with me, I might have some direct skill that would relate, something that we haven't discussed yet."

Oh yes, she was impressive. She eventually won the little war of words, as Zach opened up slightly about the LakeShore project, and she proceeded to point out some very valid reasons why it made sense for him to consider her.

Finally, he stood to show her to the door, explaining his procedures and that he would contact her after concluding the interviews. He gestured with a gentle hand, leading her to the door, but ever careful not to touch. Taylor turned, smiled and thanked him for his time as she left the room. Zach watched her walk down the hallway to the door. As he turned away, he noticed John's secretary glaring distastefully. Trying to salvage the situation, he grinned callously and returned to the privacy of his office.

She was quite a woman, this Taylor Williams. He was afraid that his interest lay more in her than in her potential as the new member of his team. But it was true, she was also well qualified. He believed she could do the job. Could he work with her though? Without a conflict of interest? He told himself yes. Zach had never believed in office romances; that's when things got screwed up. But on the other hand, he couldn't hire someone else not as qualified just because he was attracted to this woman. He would ignore it and hire Taylor to benefit his programming team, or so he convinced himself.

Zach interviewed several more that afternoon, but his mind was already made up. He was hiring Taylor Williams. None of them were as qualified anyway, so it didn't matter. . . did it?

If her references checked out, he would have Personnel call Taylor that evening and make a verbal offer.

Later Zach found himself roaming an empty apartment again. His mind had been on her all evening. He didn't want to admit it, but she was there, in every other thought that raced through his head. Lucky for Zach though, it had been a long day, having been tacked onto a longer night before. He was exhausted and drifting off before 9:00. As he stumbled into the bedroom, he looked around at its emptiness. It had plush white carpet and beige walls around the raised king size pedestal bed. Its outside wall was full glass, just as the living room. As attractive as it was, it could use a woman's touch. Enough already, he told himself and turned out the light.

Chapter Three

When Zachery pulled into the parking lot it was 6:15. He found a spot and quickly parked his car. As he walked towards the entrance, he scanned the lot for Bob's car. There it was, that ugly boat. In the far corner, away from the other cars, a white 1979 Cadillac El Dorado was parked in two spots. . .so big that it required both.

Zach ducked under the low hanging awning and entered the restaurant. It was one of those yuppie style restaurant/pub chains that had become so popular in the last several years. He spotted his friend by a window and joined him.

"Nice hat," Zach said, not sure if he really meant it or was just being sarcastic to his friend.

His reference was to an off-white cowboy hat that rested on the man's head.

"Thanks, buddy," the man said with a country boy drawl.

"Why didn't you wear that into the office today?" Zach joked.

"I didn't want to put up with your crap," the man answered. "I left it in the car."

"Yeah, I saw it out there," Zach changed the subject. "When are you gonna sell that boat and get a real car?"

"Boat, hell," Bob laughed, then pointed out the window to his Caddy. "That there's a classic, my friend. They don't build'em like that no more. That's true American right there."

"Okay. . .okay," Zach chuckled.

Bob was Zach's right hand man. He was an excellent programmer and manager, which was how he had earned his position on Zachery's team. But at times, he could be a bit eccentric. He was very tall and skinny with thick blonde hair and wore a conservative business suit. But instead of the normal dress shoes you might expect, he sported snakeskin cowboy boots. This hat was just a bonus. He usually didn't go that far at the office.

With his country look and sound, he seemed like he might just as easily have been a rodeo rider rather than a brilliant computer programmer in one of the largest cities in the country. His unconventional look had affectionately earned Bob his nickname of "Cowboy Bob."

"What's goin' on these days?" Zach asked his friend.

"Not much," Cowboy replied. "I'm s'pposed to go see a quarterhorse tomorrow. The price is right. If it ain't no run down nag, I'll probably buy her."

"How many will that make?"

"If I get her, she'll be the sixth."

"How's Edie?" Zach continued politely.

"Oh, the old lady's fine. Doin' the same old thing."

"Shopping?"

"Shopping," Bob shook his head as they both enjoyed a laugh at his wife's expense.

A waitress came to the table as they were settling down. She wore very high cut white shorts and a bright green crop top T-shirt. Zach took a quick double take at her as she pulled a pen from behind her ear. She had long wavy dark hair that she flipped aside while removing the pen. He looked at Bob, who was amused by Zach's obvious approval of her looks. They each ordered a cocktail, and she whisked away.

"There ya go man," Bob prodded. "She looks mighty fine from my point a' view."

"Yeah," Zach acknowledged. "She's cute, isn't she?"

"How long's it been since you been out on a date?"

"Too long."

"Really? How long?"

"I don't know," Zach answered. "Probably three or four months. Why? What do you care?"

"Why?" Bob sounded confused. "There's tons of women out there that'd go out with you."

"I've been busy. . .you know, with the Mexicana Shipping project. Just haven't had any time."

"You're gonna have to lighten up, pardner. You work too hard."

"I know. You say that every time I see you."

"Yes I do," Cowboy shook his finger at Zach. "And I'm right every time I say it! You're gonna have to slow down and enjoy life a little. There's always gonna be another project, but you're not gonna be young forever."

"Okay, I give up."

"Take this little girl here, for instance." Bob nodded towards their waitress. "She looks like a nice wholesome girl."

Zach chuckled as he eyed the waitress's wholesome legs.

"We'll see," Zach decided to change the subject. "What do you want to eat?"

"I think I'll have one a' them half-pound burgers," Bob answered as he looked back to the menu. "What about you?"

"I'm getting the barbecue salad."

"Hey, you want a' split an order of chicken wings?"

"Wings? You know me. I love wings."

"Good," Bob closed his menu. "Extra hot."

"God man," Zach winced. "You're gonna kill me with this hot food yet."

The waitress returned to the table with their drinks. As they ordered the food, Bob watched Zachery, waiting for his move. But he did nothing, not even flirt. Cowboy shook his head disapprovingly as they watched her tight rear twisting away.

"Boy. . .she is hot," Bob started. "I don't know what your problem is, boy. If I was single, I'd."

"That's the problem," Zach interrupted. "You've been married too long."

"What's that supposed to mean?"

"It means that I was going to say something to her, but I noticed she had a ring on." He paused to make his point. "She's married."

"Oh," Bob mumbled. "I didn't even notice."

"Yeah, you married guys forget about that kind of stuff."

"Boy. . ." Cowboy pondered. "I guess I'm out a' practice, huh?"

Zach shook his head and raised the glass to his lips for a drink.

"Is there any reason you wanted to get together tonight?" Bob asked after a long silence.

"Well, as a matter of fact, there is."

"Okay. What is it?"

"It's about work."

"Damn, I knew it. You've got a one track mind, man, and I think your train done derailed off it."

"Don't worry." Zach said. "It's not a big deal. I just wanted to make you aware of some things, and I thought we could get together since it's been so long."

"Well, you're right there," Bob joked. "We haven't been out together in months."

"Excuse me, gentlemen," the waitress interrupted. "Here is your appetizer."

She sat the wings in the center of the table as Zach caught a hint of the aroma.

"God almighty, those smell strong," he said.

"You did order extra hot, didn't you?" asked the waitress.

"They're fine darlin'," Bob jumped in, pulling the tray closer as if protecting it.

As they ate, Zach related the story to Bob, between putting out the wing–induced fire in his mouth, gulping down several beers. Zach told Bob of his meeting with John and how he had been promoted. After a congratulation from Bob, he continued with the story of the LakeShore account, how big the project was, how much revenue it meant to Global and, most of all, how the timeframe was so tight.

After dinner, Zach brought the last subject up.

"What do you think?" Zach asked him.

"You're talkin' alot a' work. You think we can get it done on time?"

"I think so," Zach stated confidently. "I've been working on the project plan, and I think the timeline looks good. I'm planning to brief everyone at the next staff meeting."

"Okay, if you say so. . ."

"One more thing, Bob."

"What's that, bub?"

"I'm really going to need you on this one. As tight as the schedule looks, I'll be pretty busy myself. I'd like you to take a more active role in managing the team. I want you to make sure we don't fall behind. . .LakeShore or us."

"Sure," Bob was a bit puzzled. "You know I will, if that's what ya need."

"I guess I'm trying to tell you that I want you to act as the team leader."

"But I thought Berringer said you were still the team leader?" Cowboy questioned.

"Yeah, but I won't have as much time for the day to day, and I need to get out of it if I'm gonna do my job right."

"Okay, whatever you want." It was the only thing Bob knew to say.

"I'm going to give you a pay increase along with this, Bob. I don't know about the title yet. If it turns out that I'm never available as the team leader, I'll make sure that you get the title to go with it. But for now, let's leave it like this, at least through this LakeShore thing."

"Great," Bob hadn't been expecting anything. "And hell, the title don't mean nothin' to me. You know that. Just give me the money any day. Mo money!"

"All right then, it's settled." Zach smiled. "I'll announce it to everyone else at the staff meeting."

"I guess I'm caught up on everything now, huh?" Bob asked, stunned.

"That ought to do it."

"And I thought I knew what was goin' on. Things move fast around here, don't they?"

The young lady in the white shorts dropped their checks at the table. They watched her wiggle off again, sighing.

"Now, Zach. . ." Cowboy was making another point judging from the tone of his voice. "I want you to listen to what I said."

"What's that?" Zach asked the question even though he already knew the answer.

"You start gettin' out more, bub. You're pissin' your life away for Global. . .and for what?"

"What's wrong with Global?" Zach had taken offense to the statement.

"Nothin'. I like hard work and good money as much as the next guy. . .Maybe not in that order. But the point is, you gotta have your own life, 'cause if ya don't, someday you're gonna wake up and see an old fart in the mirror. And ya won't have anybody. You'll be all alone."

"Okay," Zach stopped him. "That's enough of the lecture. I know you're right. As soon as this LakeShore thing is over, I'll take some time and relax."

"As soon as this LakeShore thing, huh?" Bob asked rhetorically. He knew he was talking to a brick wall. "We'll see."

But Zach did listen. There were times now when he was lonely. He made lots of money but had no one to spend it on. He was a powerful man at work, giving orders to subordinates, but without a soul at home to even talk to. What would it be like in 10 years? 20 years? Or even 30? The loneliness would only compound. Maybe Bob was right. Global was wonderful, but he wouldn't always have them. They were like a family, but even families couldn't always be there for you.

Chapter

Four

Just outside of town, a lone dark sedan cruised north on a deserted two lane highway. The car was running slightly above the speed limit, but slow enough not to attract unwanted attention if a cop were to emerge from a shadowy side road. The driver was alone. He checked the rearview mirror now and then for no apparent reason. His face was plump, gruff cheeks and double chin hanging loosely from neglect over the years. He tugged at a leather belt where his gut hung over considerably. Dark corn fields lined both sides of the straight road. The time was late, after midnight. The driver rubbed his eyes and the dark circles under them. It was a cloudy night, extremely dark without the moon breaking through, while to the east, an occasional lightning bolt lit the horizon. Probably out over Lake Michigan, he thought glancing that way.

Finally, after 30 minutes, he slowed as the car approached a turnoff. His eyes glanced up, checking the mirror one last time for traffic. Nothing. . .the usual. He slowed to a stop outside a chain link fence surrounding a warehouse. Pointing the headlights to the center of the gates, he lumbered around the front of the car and used the light to help find the keyhole and unlock them. He drove through, closed the fence behind him, then drove to the corner of the large metal building. This was the only structure on the property. At the closest corner of the building was a single metal door with a light over it. This was the only source of light on the entire structure.

He grabbed a briefcase from the passenger seat and entered the building through the door, relocking it behind him. It was dark and completely silent inside. He fumbled around on the wall until a switch was found. It illuminated the middle of the building where there was an opening, but did little for the perimeter which was all lined with tall metal shelving. A faint noise caught his attention when the lights came on. Two large rats scurried behind the tall metal shelving several rows down. They turned back to him, shocking a gasp from his lungs when their eyes briefly glowed red from the reflecting light.

"Goddamn rats," he murmured to himself and started down a row toward the center of the building. "Why in the hell am I doing this here anyway? I need to find some better working conditions!"

He walked across the open area to the back wall of the building. A wooden stairway led to a few offices that overlooked the interior of the warehouse. He rambled up the steps, pausing at the top to catch his breath, and entered the last door down the plankway.

It was a plain office. A green metal desk sat in the middle of the 10' x 10' room. Behind it was a matching credenza with a computer terminal sitting on top. The chubby man walked around the desk and plopped down in the chair. He turned to face the computer screen, flipped the switch on and leaned back as it came to life. After a few keystrokes, he whirled around to the desk and opened the briefcase. It was filled with folders and various labeled disks. He pulled the top folder out and spread its contents on the desktop before discarding it. The label stuck to the top corner read LAKESHORE NATIONAL BANK PROJECT. The files contained seemingly everything you would ever want to know about the bank. There were reports on all key officers and managers, even board members. Other reports revealed financial portfolios of bank customers: the big corporations with a dozen accounts and millions of dollars funneling through daily, the rich people, collecting interest on fat savings accounts filled to their insurable limits. If it was a lot of money, it was in these reports.

The ugly man closely examined most of the documents. He was very thorough, making notes on some papers, highlighting sections of others, etc. He seemed to be a professional type considering his approach to work, but then again, he had obnoxious mannerisms, scratching himself and belching loudly as he rammed different snacks into his mouth.

After almost an hour of this, he turned back to the computer terminal behind him. His fat little hands moved freely to the keyboard. It seemed something of a mismatch. He just didn't look the computer part. He typed a few words out and pressed the enter key. A moment later the screen displayed in large bold print 'WELCOME TO THE GLOBAL NETWORK. . .PLEASE ENTER YOUR PASSWORD NOW:_'. He grinned slightly, as he typed his answer. The terminal immediately flashed a bright red message 'INVALID USER,' but just as quickly, it was gone. Another message followed it, 'THANK YOU. . .LOGIN IS NOW COMPLETE' indicating that the unknown man was now fully connected to Global Computer Solutions' private computer network.

He typed at a lightning pace, obviously familiar with what he was doing. Columns of files flashed onto his screen as he asked for them. His eyes squinted while he paused and looked for a particular file. Finally, he found one that drew his attention. The hands stroked out another command to load it so he could examine its contents. When the file came up, it was apparent that this was a program file. At the top, a paragraph explained its purpose, author and the client Global had written it for. The client was a bank, but not the LakeShore Bank listed on the folders.

The man continued. He paged through screen after screen of computer language instructions. His fluency showed as he found a specific spot in the program and began typing changes to it. Line after line, page after page, his keystrokes were changing the logic and purpose of this program. He worked feverishly, finishing that after several hours, only to find another program, another victim, load it and begin altering its commands.

At 4:30 A.M., the man's pace was slowing. He had been at it for four hours without a break. His eyes were red and even puffier than before. They had a dazed look.

Suddenly, a shrill ringing broke through the silence causing the man to jump back from the terminal. His eyes were wide open now, frightened awake by the noise.

"Shit," he exclaimed aloud.

The ringing burst out again. He deduced with this second time, that it was just a telephone. He turned to the phone on the wall next to the office door and gave it a dirty look. Should he answer it? Surely it wasn't a normal call, not at 4:30 in the morning. It must be them. But why would they be calling now? He decided to answer it quietly and try to recognize the voice. While it rang a third time, he cautiously walked towards it, then picked up the receiver and put it to his ear without speaking.

"Hello," a voice rang through. There was a long pause. "Hello. . .it's just me."

The man finally answered after listening to the voice.

"Hello! What the hell are you calling now for?"

"I just woke up. I thought I'd see how you were doing," the caller said.

"I got started," the fat man answered. "But it's a little early to tell."

"You know what kind of time frame we're working with," the caller insisted.

"YES, I know," the fat man snapped back.

"Okay, okay."

"Did you call for any particular reason?"

"No. . .Just wanted to see if you had everything you needed." The caller was referring to the folders.

"Yeah, for now. I'm just doing preliminary coding right now anyway," he said as he rummaged through the loose papers scattered on the desk.

"Well, I was just nervous about this schedule," the caller began. "If we're going to do this, we have to keep up."

"You know how it works. . .I can't tell anything just yet. I'll give you a status report in two weeks." Again the fat man was annoyed with the caller. But the caller was not intimidated.

"Fine! You do that. But don't fall behind on this one."
There was a long silence before the caller finished. "I'll get
you a copy of the detailed project plan as soon as Mr.
Crawford completes it. It should be nearly finished. He's
supposed to present it in his next staff meeting."

"All right," the fat man said, backing down somewhat.
"I'll need it ASAP."

"You better wrap it up and get out of there before
anyone shows early for work."

"You're right. We really don't need that."

"Talk to you in a few days?" the caller inquired brashly.

"You know where to find me," the fat man smarted back
to him and hung up, shaking his head.

He went to the computer and began saving his programming changes. It only took a minute. Checking his
watch, 4:50, he slowed his pace and finished off a bag of
potato chips as he relaxed. There shouldn't be anyone
around for another hour. Chips gone, his bloated little hand
turned off the computer and began packing up the papers.
Grease from his fingers stained a few of them. He took no
notice.

Everything was packed, and he glanced around the
room once before turning off the light and pulling the door
closed behind him. He retraced all his steps carefully. This
location was somewhat new, better be careful not to leave
anything up to chance. In the middle part of the building, he
looked back up to the room he had been using. It was
indeed dark, door closed, stairway lights off. Again at the
door, one last look over, and he flipped the switches causing
complete darkness to fall over the warehouse floor. The
heavy door rumbled through the corridors of steel shelving
when it was slammed shut.

A hint of light in the east meant that it would soon be
daybreak. The fat man worried just a little about not having
left earlier. Soon workers would fill this place, and he had to
be gone before the very first one arrived. He quickly walked
to his car and hopped in. Time to get out of there, he told
himself.

The car spun around, kicking up loose gravel and dust
as the driver nervously held the gas down too far. The
wheels locked in front of the chain link gates. He slammed
them open and drove through to the other side, then swung

them closed again, fastened the padlock and took off. The tires screeched loudly when they hit the pavement of the road, but he paid no attention.

His eyes checked all mirrors in the car. He saw no one. The road was still deserted. The daylight grew stronger by the second. Suddenly, he spotted something in the distance with the rearview mirror. *'Oh no!'* he thought to himself. A set of red and blue lights flashed in the distance. A state trooper was closing on him at a tremendous rate. He looked around in a state of panic. The police car was getting closer. His fat hand reached between his legs under the seat and found a small handgun. He placed it in the seat beside him. In only a few short moments, the cop was almost on the bumper of his sedan. The fat man stared intently into the mirror, eyeing the face of the policeman, the outline of his straight brimmed hat. The cop had caught up to him. He drove on defiantly, but as quickly as he had appeared, he disappeared. The lights swung to the side, out of sight from his mirror. Then they zipped by him on the way to some other emergency, not after him at all. He watched the tail lights soar out of sight in the next few seconds, looked down at the briefcase and the gun lying beside it.

"Shit. . .fuckin' paranoid!" he mumbled aloud and began laughing thunderously.

Chapter
Five

Several days later, Zach was pleasantly surprised to find Taylor waiting for him in the lobby when he arrived at work. He took a deep breath and walked over to her. "Good morning, Ms. Williams," he said.

"Good morning," she replied. "And, please. . .Taylor."

"I thought you had another job," Zach stated, somewhat puzzled. He'd known that she accepted the offer but didn't expect her so quickly.

"Well, I did, but when I told them that I was leaving, they got upset and told me the notice wouldn't be necessary."

"I don't want you to leave your employer. . .former employer in a bind," Zach offered. "I mean, if one of my employees. . ."

"I offered to stay long enough to train my replacement," she interrupted. She didn't want Zach to think she'd jumped ship. "My boss said the night operator would do both our jobs until they found someone. He wasn't happy at all."

"Well, anyway, I'm glad you're here. I have a meeting with my team this morning to brief them on this new project."

Zach was delighted to see her again so quickly. "I think you need to be there anyway. After the meeting, I'll show you to your office, and you can get started on all those personnel forms."

She smiled back at him. He extended his arm and gestured for her to come with him to the conference room. Her dress was slightly more conservative this morning, but she still looked stunning. Today, she wore a gray checkered skirt with matching jacket and a creme colored blouse underneath, very professional. Zach led her down the hall, almost putting his hand against the small of her back, but quickly realized it would be out of line. Boy, it HAD been a long time, hadn't it? He opened a heavy glass door leading into a conference room. It was a brightly lit room with glass walls and blinds to close off the rest of the office. A podium and whiteboard were at the front, facing five rows of chairs in the middle of the room. A group of men and women sat scattered around the room. They ranged in age from mid-twenties to about forty. One of the men, Bob, poked through a box of doughnuts sitting on a table to the side.

Zach entered the room, introducing Taylor to the group. It appeared that at least several were skeptical about her. Zach wasn't too worried about what they were thinking; he had the distinct impression that she could handle herself just fine.

With everyone present, Zach called the meeting to order. He began by telling the group about Taylor, her background and what responsibilities she had, as well as explaining all of his team's duties to her. Zachery really felt that he had a good team, and his pride in them showed. Everyone worked together to get the job done, and everyone sacrificed together when it was crunch time. It was tough to put together a good team in this business. With the pressure of nearing deadlines and seemingly impossible technical hurdles, it took a certain type of person to do this work. So, building a complete team of people that have the skills, can handle that pressure and, most of all, get along with each other, was quite a task indeed.

Other managers had tried to take his people for their project, but Zach always went to bat for his team. He didn't want it broken up.

Each had his own role to fulfill. The team was comprised of a widely varying group of programmers. Each had his or her own little niche or specialty. Zach had stolen one of his senior guys from a big six accounting firm. The accounting background and methodologies had proved invaluable in many projects. Another member, a middle aged woman, had come to Global with the Indiana bank project. Before that she had been an independent contractor with considerable banking experience. Several other programmers with different levels of experience made up the rest of the team, except for the specialty folks. A DBA (database administrator), systems guy and education specialist rounded out the team. All of these talents complemented each other, combining to build a very close knit team.

Zach knew just that. He was proud and lucky to have such a good group of talented people. He was just as confident that Taylor would also live up to these standards.

As he hooked his notebook computer to the projector, Zach began going over the preliminary project plan with his colleagues. Each task was laid out with the precision and expertise that only Zach Crawford could have designed.

They would work on Global's in-house computer system until all of the testing on LakeShore's new system was completed and the system was ready. After he was satisfied with the equipment setup, he would link into the bank from Global's network. This link was a standard practice of the company. It helped speed the project, as well as give ongoing support services long after the work was completed. The T1 line was already ordered and in the queue. A small group would then go on-site to install the applications and train bank personnel. As the project neared completion, Global assisted in the development of an implementation plan and finally the actual cutover. It was a fairly normal plan. All of Global's projects were structured similarly, with a standard methodology but ever varying details. Zach illustrated all the points, drawing out the normal timelines and dependencies as he went.

About twenty minutes into the meeting, John walked in through a rear door and took a seat at the very back, crossing his legs. This seemed a bit odd to Zachery because John usually didn't take a direct interest in very many projects. As a matter of fact, he could only remember one other project since he'd been there that John had been involved in, and that one was the first project that John had given him to manage. But that didn't change the fact that there he was in the back, listening, even taking notes on a couple of points as Zach continued. It was probably just the visibility of the project that brought John's attention. After all, Global stood to make nearly a million dollars on the deal or lose its reputation if things went sour. After a deep breath and a pause, Zach continued with the meeting, paying no heed to John in the back of the room.

Meanwhile, in the front, Taylor sat with her arms and legs crossed, watching Zach intently. She saw the self confidence, the leadership qualities which Zach possessed, and it impressed her. He talked with authority and strength. She liked this; he was a man in control of his life, one who knew how to get what he wanted. As the meeting continued, Taylor found herself admiring him as she watched and listened. Reflections of lights glistened in his hair as he moved about. He was quite a motivator. It was easy to see that his team respected him deeply.

But several times she caught herself thinking about how handsome he was. This was definitely not a good thing. She had never believed in office romance, especially getting involved with your boss. Being labeled the slut who fucked her way up the company ladder was not the way to start a new job. She forced the thoughts out, trying to concentrate on the task at hand, her new career.

After nearly two hours the meeting adjourned, and Zach was ready for a break. His voice harsh and gruff from two hours of speech, he asked if there were any questions before scheduling a project status meeting for the same time next week.

With the meeting over, Zach made his way back to John. "Good morning, John," he said. "It's a surprise to see you here."

"Yes, Zach my boy, I like to get involved in some of the larger projects," He spoke with a slight southern drawl.

"Involved, John?" Zachery asked.

"I just wanted to listen in and keep tabs on what's going on, get a better feel for the schedule. I don't mean to interfere with your work; it's your project to manage. Like I said, son, lot of visibility on this one. I need to be more knowledgeable about the details in case I get put on the spot sometime." As he turned to the door, John added, "By the way, I was very impressed with the meeting, Zach."

"Thanks, John. I just hope I covered everything, haven't forgotten any details."

"Oh, you're fine. Quit worrying."

"That's what you pay me for, John," Zach chuckled.

"Okay, Zach, you have a good day."

"You, too. Good-bye, John."

Later that afternoon, Zach found himself sitting in the plush leather chair behind the desk in his new office. But he wasn't wasting any time. After grabbing a few papers and a scratch pad, he swung the chair around facing the computer on the credenza. It sat perched there like the silent partner, waiting for an assignment.

Zach reached his hands out and gently pulled the keyboard to a comfortable position. He knew that he couldn't waste time, not on this project. It was time to get LakeShore involved. The quicker they were responsible, the better for him. The first step in that process was to establish a means of communicating, which always meant generating a status report. And the first was always the most difficult. Diplomacy was often the name of the game in this area. How do you tell someone who's paying YOU a ton of money that this is the long list of things that THEY have to do for you? And if they don't do those things when you want them done, there will be consequences.

Luckily, this was one of Zach Crawford's fortes. He was from the old school, where hard work and honesty still played a role. Invariably, Global's clients saw this in him and quickly gained respect for him. It was very important, for if it didn't happen, they would fight every step of the way. He'd seen it happen too many times in his years with Global.

By the time Zach came up for air, it was already well after six o'clock. His eyes were swollen and red. It was time to call it a day. He wrapped things up, saved his work and left.

It wasn't until he reached the elevator that Zach realized he'd forgotten his day planner. He would need it if he was to finish the status report that evening. He turned and was staring at the entry doors to the computer room. I realize this security stuff is necessary, he thought to himself, but it can be a pain in the ass sometimes, too. He punched in his security code and reached over to yank on the door, but it wouldn't open. He yanked harder, then tried his code a second time. It still wouldn't budge.

"What in the hell is wrong with this thing?" he said aloud. His security code was supposed to allow him through the doors any time of the day or night.

He glanced down at his wrist; nearly 7:30, later than he thought. Damn. Now, he couldn't finish. Guess it'll have to wait until morning.

Zach turned to face the elevator and met a guard on the other side of the opening door. At first he was startled, but then recognized him as one of the regulars. Why did this seem so strange to Zachery? He couldn't quite place the reason, but something was a little bit strange. The guard was unaware of why Mr. Crawford's security might be screwed up and quickly let the executive back in.

Later in the evening, Zach lay resting between the soft satin sheets of his bed listening to the radio playing softly in the background. Dim lights illuminated the huge master bedroom with its raised king size bed. The day planner lay on the bed beside him, still open. Suddenly, it hit him. The reason the incident with the door seemed so strange to him was because the guards usually weren't even there yet at that time of the day. They don't come in until 9:00. As many late nights as he put in, he should know. Odd, he thought, but who knows. Maybe security was stepped up recently. But that still didn't explain why his code wouldn't work, or why he wasn't told about it. Even his old clearance, before the promotion should get him in at 7:30 in the evening. Those goons in sys-admin must've fucked up his account when they tried to change it.

It was a good day, he told himself. There's no reason to get pissed about this. Under the smooth sheets, he shifted his lean body and then his thoughts.

Taylor Williams. A mental note...Check with her in the morning to see if she had experienced any problems on her first day. He looked forward to it. She fascinated him already. How was he to maintain a working relationship with such an irresistible young woman? How long could he resist pursuing his attraction to her?

Shifting again, he raised his arms to rest behind his head. A slow easy jazz melody, something by Kenny G, he thought, lulled him into a peaceful sleep.

The peacefulness, however, didn't last. There was the dream, that same damn dream, coming back to haunt him once again. The campfire burned with the wood crackling and popping below the louder noises of the drunken group. It was the same scene, exactly as before. They jumped up, Zach and the other boys, dragging the one that had been bound further into the dark woods. They walked quickly down a small dark path with only a few dim flashlights to lead their way. The young Zachery and his friends pulled and yanked on the young boy purposely, laughing and tormenting him. By now the whole group was so drunk that they stumbled over each other and weaved on and off of the path as they tried to walk. Finally, the path ended, turning into a patch of short, thick undergrowth. This undergrowth surrounded a small dirt clearing with two to three small trees scattered about. The new moon poured its bright light over them. They pulled the young boy to a larger tree in the center of the field and unbound him for a moment. One of his wrists was bleeding from the yanking and pulling during the trip through the woods.

The boy opposite Zach laughed and whispered, "You'd better hope nothin' gets a whiff of that. You know there's all kinds of wild animals scattered through these woods." Zach wrapped the boy's arms around the tree and tried to gently re-tie the ropes to the boy's bleeding wrists. He winced slightly as the rough grain of the rope grated at his injuries, but he wasn't complaining. They all gathered around the boy with the leader stepping toward him to speak.

He pushed the long blonde hair out of his eyes and smiled at the boy. "Okay, boy, you know what you have to do. You have to get loose from there and be back at the campus by dawn. If you make it, you're one of us. If you don't. . .," he paused and laughed wildly for what seemed like an endless amount of time. "If you don't, you better hope that someone finds you before you starve to death wrapped around this tree."

He reached into his pocket and fumbled around for a moment before pulling out a whistle with a small chain around it. Then he paused and took a long guzzle of his brew before breaking it against a rock, and finally leaned down face to face with the boy.

"Now, here's the whistle," the leader said sarcastically as he wrapped the whistle around the boy's neck. "This is your only other chance; when we walk away from here, if you fuckin' pussy out, you'd better blow this god damn whistle before we're too far away to hear it. We hear the whistle, we come untie you, take you home, and we never wanna see your fagot ass again. If not, hope to see you in the morning."

He laughed again, then rammed the whistle in the boy's mouth. "Now don't sneeze and blow that whistle out of your mouth, 'less you can put it back with your toes."

The whole group cackled. The leader waved his hand wildly, and they scattered into the woods like field mice, several of them stumbling and laughing out of sight.

"Let's go guys."

At that, Zach jumped up. The satin sheets were soaking wet with sweat. . .yet again. His heart pounded hard in his chest, harder in his ears, and his breath was short as if he had been running a race. He used one of the sheets to wipe the dripping sweat from his clammy face and forehead. Then Zach dropped his face into his hands, disgusted that he couldn't shake it.

Once again it was early morning, and Zach Crawford, a young man with seemingly everything he could ever need or want, sat at the foot of his bed like a helpless frightened child hunching over with his head buried between his hands.

He knew he wouldn't sleep the rest of the night, but instead roam an empty apartment looking for something to keep his mind busy, something to keep him from dwelling on the terrible nightmare he was experiencing.

But morning was always a magical time. The bright sunshine always washed away the fears, the pains of the night for Zach. Things would be better then.

Chapter
Six

Zach's face was pale, and his eyes red and bloodshot from the rough night before. He looked very tired. Being tired didn't bother Zach very much, though. He'd gotten used to it. For much of his adult life, the dreams would come and wake him in the night. The dreams were no mystery. They were an outlet for Zach's subconscious mind, some sort of terrible secret that he tried to keep suppressed in his past, a memory so terrible that he couldn't face it.

With morning upon him, Zach went about business as usual. The morning brought light and hope, and things didn't seem as bad. It was something that every child has experienced, but few adults still dealt with after maturing. The sun would be bright, and he could look up into the blue sky and somehow push all the bad stuff out of his head for yet another day.

On the patio Zach breathed the cool morning air deeply into his lungs. It felt good. He felt better. The sun had risen, and activity filled the streets below. Zach scanned his surroundings and considered what a lucky man he was.

Slowly he fell into the normal routine as the dream subsided. Sitting at the dining table, Zach flipped through the daily paper. The business and sports sections were his usual interests. As he flipped through the pages, a picture caught his eye in the "Local Profiles" section of the business section. He had to take a double take. It was him! The heading read, "Global Computer Solutions Executive promoted." The article named Zachery Crawford as new Regional Project Director and continued with a few paragraphs of his record with the company. He read it several more times, not sure how he should react. It wasn't a big deal, he told himself. Yet, he couldn't help feeling proud. It seemed juvenile to make a big deal out of it, but it did feel good. They say that everyone is famous for 15 minutes, and this must be his.

Zach carefully folded the paper so that it might be put away and saved, something to look back on as his "Glory Days."

As Zach came into the offices, he was stopped by a secretary. She was a cute young brunette, working as a co-op from her senior year at high school. She waved him down before he entered the elevator. She loved the chance to talk and flirt with Zach.

"Mr. Crawford," she was yelling as he stopped and made a detour to the front counter. Maybe she had seen the article.

He glanced over her young vivacious body. God, she was gorgeous. How could she be only 17? Her slight advances caught his attention as she tried to edge a little closer to him.

"Yes, Kathy?" he answered.

"Uh Zach," she started, mustering up her best sensual voice. "Your brother called this morning, and when you weren't here, he said that he would try to catch you at home."

A frown came across Zach's face, diverting his attention from her playful eyes which were peering so deeply into his.

"Kathy, I don't have a brother."

"You don't?" Her expression immediately changed. It was her first job, and she was very apprehensive concerning any mistakes she might make. "Oh no, he said that he was your brother."

"Well, what happened?" Zach asked kindly so as not to alarm her any worse.

"He called and asked for you, and when I told him that you weren't here, he asked for your number and said he would try to catch you at home."

"And did you give it to him?"

"Well, not at first," she answered while her flirting eyes had begun to water up, about to burst into tears. "I told him that we weren't allowed to give out any information like that. That's when he told me he was your brother. . .said he was gonna surprise you. I went ahead and gave it to him then. I'm sorry sir, I didn't know. Please forgive me. I'm really sorry."

"That's okay, Kathy, it's probably just a salesman or something. He thought he'd catch me off guard at home. Just don't give any information like that out again."

"Yes sir, I'm sorry. It won't happen again. I promise!"

"Don't worry about it."

Zachery gave her a reassuring pat on the back which seemed to calm her somewhat. As he continued to the sixth floor, he thought of what he might say to a salesman ballsy enough to call him at home. He delighted in the difficulty he would send his way if the call were to come.

In the computer room everything was already buzzing. In the corner printers hammered off sheet after sheet of paper. The disk drives on the other side of the room were purring away. Standing in the middle of the room, of course, were the processors, humming away, hundreds of words scrolling up display screens on the tables beside them. Two men stood hovered over one of these screens on the table, examining page after page of a programming printout. The two were on his programming team and had been in yesterday's briefing. They had spent practically an hour now trying to track down a bug in this program.

"Hey Zach, can you come here for a minute?" one of the men yelled.

"Sure, what do you need, Jerry?" Zach asked as he walked over to join the two men.

The one that had yelled, Jerry, was older than Zach, maybe thirty-five. He had dark hair, and his hairline was definitely receding. In response to Zach's question, he gestured angrily at the piles of paper on the table.

"This program is hozed, man. Can you take a look at it?"

"Zach," said the other man, with a western drawl.

The other man was Cowboy Bob. He wore a conservative suit, but sported pointed snake-skin cowboy boots, very typical. He began to fill Zach in on the problem.

"Yeah, yeah, Bob," he answered jokingly. "What have you guys done now?"

"Zach," he repeated after a pause. "We've got a problem here. We've written a routine to do an amortization schedule for mortgage loans at the bank, but it ain't figurin' right. We've gone over and over the calculations, and they look fine, so I can't see what's been done wrong. It's just got me all bum-fuzzled."

This team had spent alot of time with their boss and knew his roots with the company. Zach had earned a fine reputation as a technical guru in his earlier years with Global. It was probably one of the reasons he was so well respected. Unlike so many managers who wouldn't know a "byte" if it bit them on the ass, he understood the challenges his people faced, and they knew it.

"What're you guys asking me for?" Zach joked.

"We know you're above this sort of thing now. . .but, maybe you could grace us with some of your brilliance."

They all enjoyed a chuckle at Zach's expense.

"Here, let me take a look at it," he finally offered.

He bent down, resting his hands on the table and began looking through the many lines of code. The other man, who had remained silent until now, leaned down and pointed on the paper.

"See here, here, and here is where the calculations are," he mumbled.

Zach glanced momentarily at the calculations before looking off. He knew these two men well enough to know that if they thought the calculations were right, then they were probably right. Besides that, it would take him quite a long time to figure out if they were right anyway.

Zach pulled a chair up backwards and straddled it. He began following the program step by step from the first calculation to where it was printed on paper. Occasionally, he flipped toward the front of the program, checking the definitions of the different names and items they had used in the routine. After five or six minutes, he had the answer, but double checked himself before saying anything.

After he was sure, he pointed and said strongly, "There! There it is." He was pointing at a particular line in the program. The two men leaned down closer to see.

"What is it?" Bob asked.

"Yeah, what's wrong with that?" replied the other.

"I know, I know what you're thinking," answered Zach, having anticipated their impulsive skepticism. "But, here's what happened. Look. After you have an answer to your second calculation here, you move it to a new area of memory in order to do the next calculation. The new area is smaller than the original one, so when you move it there, you're dropping off part of the number. You're still performing the calculation correctly, but with the wrong information."

Bob and his older sidekick sighed with disgust, realizing they had wasted an hour on such an easy problem. Zach had trusted their abilities, where they had questioned themselves on the calculation, completely overlooking this simpler explanation.

"Thanks for the help," they both echoed and quickly scribbled down the necessary changes to make in this new light.

Zachery stood and looked up from the table where his eyes met Taylor's. She was standing across the room, staring straight at him. He looked back at her for a moment and then started to turn away.

Even when he was much younger, Zach had never been any good at this game. It wasn't that he didn't know what was going on. Back in school, he and his friends used to kid each other about these things. What he was receiving now from Taylor was what they had called "the look." Yes, Taylor was giving him "the look," as strong and effective a means of flirtation as any other, and all without having to say a word. He stopped himself from looking away. If he turned now, there was no telling what impression he would leave her with. This time he would force himself to play the game. So he stared straight back into her eyes. She was beautiful.

In response, Taylor smiled toward him very slightly. Her smile seemed to reveal an innocence that made Zach feel as though she were close to him, like a very good friend even though he had only known her for a short time. But he was beginning to get short of breath, the blood rushing through him, causing his whole body to suddenly feel very hot. The game was lasting too long. Zach wasn't any good at this, his endurance short. He had already responded to her silent advance and now realized it was his move. So he broke eye contact and slowly walked over to her. The break was much needed as Zach worked on regaining his composure on the way over.

Upon reaching Taylor, he purposely took a step very close to her and brought his eyes up to hers once again.

"Good morning, Taylor," he said softly.

"Hi Zach, how are you?" she cooed back, just as softly.

He was most certainly right. It wasn't his imagination. She was making her intentions known.

"Fine, fine," Zach said, and then paused for a moment. "Is everything okay?"

"Fine, I guess," she answered still wearing that same faint smile. "Do you mean anything in particular?" she asked, speaking slowly.

Zach felt as though she were teasing him over his lack of conversation. It was like she knew exactly how he felt right now.

"No," he replied almost defensively. "How's your assignment going?" Immediately he kicked himself, wishing he could take back the stupid question.

"Oh, I'm doing fine. No problems or anything, I'm just trying to get used to this system."

Zach saw the smile leaving her face and knew he had better act fast.

"Uh, Taylor, I was thinking," he started. "I thought maybe you would like someone. . .Well, I thought maybe I could take you to dinner some night and show you around a little bit."

"I'm not really new to town, you know."

"Yeah, but I bet you haven't seen the sights in years."

"Well. . .I guess you're right. It's been a long time. I've worked very hard since moving back to the area. Not a lot of time for socializing."

"Then you're ready for a break, aren't you? Come on," he coaxed. "It'll be fine. I know I could use the break, too."

She looked down for a minute. She cursed herself, but she had started it. She couldn't back down now. When she raised her head, she was wearing that smile again.

"Okay, sure. Why not?"

He smiled back at her, "Is Friday okay?"

"Friday's fine, do you need my address?"

"Yeah, could you write it down for me?"

She ripped a corner from a sheet of a printout on the table and scribbled her name and address on it. After folding the paper over once, she gently placed the paper into his palm and closed his hand around it.

"Now, don't forget."

He waited a moment and teasingly answered, "I'll try not to."

A broad grin covered both their faces. Zach had won round two. They had forgotten about everything around them and were alone together in a crowded room. Then a voice came from nowhere, very distant at first.

"Zach," then one more time, louder. "Zach!"

Suddenly, they became aware of everything around them once again. Taylor still had his hand and, realizing it, quickly released it. She hoped that his body had blocked the view of the others in the room. She didn't need this. It would only fuel their suspicions about her. Zach turned toward the voice that had interrupted them, motioning for him to continue.

"Zach, the Tampa branch just called," the young man seemed half frantic. "They say that their on-line transaction system has been down all morning, and they're starting to get complaints from their local customers."

This was trouble! For every minute they were down, the company lost thousands of dollars, not to mention the bad publicity with its customers. Zach immediately jumped into action.

"Steve," he yelled across the room. "Get on the horn to the phone company down there and start riding them. Make sure those lines are working!" He turned back to the young man in front of him. "Call the equipment supplier for that system and tell someone to get down there and test the on-site equipment in case it's not the lines. And don't let them give you any of that finger-pointing, it's the other guy, kind of shit. I'll be in my office, I'll call Tampa; see if I can buy us some time."

He turned to Taylor momentarily. Well, he had done it. He was disappointed with himself. *'Hell. I only lasted a couple days and I'm already chasing after her,'* he thought to himself. *'Now that's willpower, isn't it? All she had to do was look my way. This is probably going to fuck everything up. I don't have time for this now. You idiot!'* he cursed himself. Without a word, he turned and left as she watched.

On the far side of the room Bob watched the scene unfold between his friend and the new girl. He wanted Zach to be happy, but was this the answer? Sure hope she doesn't have a hidden agenda, Bob considered as he watched his friend walk away.

Chapter Seven

It was only the first problem of a long stream that would consume the whole day. Zach spent most of his time on the phone arguing with suppliers and repairmen about delays and failures. By the time the day was over, Zach had done nothing at all on the LakeShore project. The only good thing that had happened all day was his meeting with Taylor, and reason told him that wasn't even necessarily so good. What would the rest of his team think? What would John think? What would he think? It could cause any number of problems. He couldn't help himself though. He was ecstatic at the thought. It had been a very long time since he had pursued a woman. Usually work took top priority, but it felt good for a change.

Zach's planner showed that he'd had a busy day scheduled. But these problems had thrown him and most of his team way behind. He knew he couldn't afford to let this project fall behind, especially fresh out of the gate.

Morning quickly turned to afternoon, and before he got a break, it was near quitting time. As he took a breather,

Zach suddenly realized he was starving. Maybe a 4:00 lunch break would refresh him.

When he returned, it was already past 5:00, and most of the building's occupants were gone for the day. He met up with a young man at the elevator door. The man was of medium height, but very small-boned. He had thick, curly dark hair, along with a thick dark beard and mustache.

"Hi, Zach," he said, his voice loud and goofy. As he spoke, his hand moved up to his nose, where he pushed up a pair of thick, dark–rimmed glasses.

Zach responded, "How are you, Cliff?" It was funny to Zach. Here was Cliff, a good programmer and very loyal worker, but he was a perfect fit of the normal stereotype given to computer gurus by the general public. In reality though, most were like anyone else, not the nerds or geeks that they were painted to be.

"Oh, I'm fine Zach. What are you doing?"

'Oh no,' Zach thought to himself. *'I can already see it coming.'* "I'm just gonna stay a little late and try to get some odds and ends done before I leave," Zach replied trying to make it sound as boring as he possibly could. It was to no avail.

"You need any help, Zach? I don't have any plans for this evening. I could stay and help. . .that way you could get done faster." Cliff had already turned his back to the elevator, evidently planning to go back in with Zach.

Zach grabbed Cliff's shoulder and gave it a firm squeeze. "Oh no, Cliff, I'll be done in no time anyway."

He turned him back around and slowly walked him into the elevator so that he could send him on his way. Cliff was still pleading and protesting to help the whole time. When the elevator doors finally separated them, Zach let out a huge sigh of relief. It wasn't that he disliked Cliff; he was nice guy and a good worker, but his personality was so nerve-racking. After the day he'd had, he couldn't take any more irritations.

Zach turned and found himself staring at the locked door leading into the computer room. He rolled his eyes and drew a deep breath before entering his code number. It worked this time! It must have been a fluke. With all the hassle of the day, yesterday's incident was forgotten until now. Why worry about it, he told himself. Seems okay today.

He walked through the double doors and into the computer room, his footsteps echoing on the white tiles. The room was empty and silent, except for the gentle whir of cooling fans. When he got to the other side, he turned and scanned it, then flipped the lights off. The only light that remained was the last of the evening daylight shining through tinted windows on one side. He walked down the hallway and into his office, shutting the door behind him.

After a glass of water, Zach took a deep breath, turned to his terminal and started to work. With everything else out of his mind, he poured himself into his work. He didn't stop for nearly three hours until the mental exhaustion started to set in, and he realized he was sitting idle. . .staring at the screen. A stream of car lights flowed past the building away from the downtown area, and slowly they began to blur into a line of light, losing their individual points. With this, Zach rubbed his burning eyes, finally admitting to himself that he was getting pretty tired.

It was almost midnight when he opened them again and realized that he was still in the office. That was a bit more rest than he had planned, but certainly nothing new. Given the hour, Zach gathered his stuff together to leave the office and headed out. The hallway was dark, except for one lone light at the far end, shining towards the computer room entrance. It was strange how the darkness seemed eerie to him. You spend so much time in an office, get so used to the surroundings, then a change like this, darkness, somehow gives it a completely different feeling.

Slowly, Zach walked away from the light. It formed a silhouette of his body against the computer room doors, strangely distorting it, from the angle of the light. His walk was slow, unsure of his movement in the dark. By the time he reached the doors, his eyes had adjusted enough to the darkness that he could now see without much problem. He reached down and opened them, moving ahead into the pitch dark computer room, with only an occasional blinking computer light to show the way.

Zach stood still for a moment, allowing his eyes to adjust a little more to this even darker room. Then, slowly again, he began walking. His footsteps echoed as they had before, though this time they seemed as if they were pounding in his head. It must be true what they say about the other senses becoming more alert when one was taken away. It certainly felt like his hearing was making up for the darkness that his eyes were experiencing.

Then he stopped short. He had heard something, a normal noise he thought, but for some reason it stood out now. He began labeling the noises coming to him. First, there were his footsteps, and then the processor cooling fans. Then there was another noise. It was the sound of the disk drives being accessed. The read-write heads were moving about, grabbing information from the platters.

That was it! That was what was wrong; he shouldn't be hearing that noise, not now. It's midnight, there shouldn't be anyone on the system. Maybe someone was here in the building working? Surely not! Everyone went home hours ago. Questions zoomed through Zach's mind. Who was it? Where was it coming from? And worst of all, what are they doing? 'Don't worry,' he told himself, but his heart was already speeding up. He jumped to the control terminals, pushing a chair aside and kneeling down. *'Calm down,'* he told himself. *'It's probably nothing. After all, I'm here, someone else could be, too.'*

His head snapped to the left examining the lights. *'Oh, shit!'* he thought to himself, not wanting to believe his eyes. Flashing lights were telling him that the activity was from outside the building. Thoughts and stories of computer whiz kids, hackers, that would alter and sabotage millions of dollars worth of information raced through his head. But how? He had designed the computer security system himself. There was no way to beat it, and if there were, it had been designed with so many levels of security that it should take months to get into this system from scratch. It should, but maybe it hadn't. Could he have made that big of a mistake as to make it this easy for an outsider to break in? His concerns suddenly grew worse. If it was a hacker, then he was responsible. After all, it was his security system. He tried to comfort himself, but paranoia had already taken control of the reins of his mind.

He looked back at the screen and started feverishly typing a command to tell him who this intruder was. The room was still dark, as Zach stared wide-eyed into the screen with the white letters reflecting in his glassy eyes. The answer rolled up the screen, listing all the operators that were supposed to be on that phone line. It showed them all inactive. . . except for the last one, the last one was active. Out from it, the message blinked "Unrecognized Operator." Zach's heart felt like it had just suddenly stopped. He knew positively now. It wasn't in his own building, and it wasn't from another branch. He looked back to the flashing lights. They were still active. It was a strange feeling that came over him, a feeling of violation. But, there was no way this person could know that he was there. What were they doing anyway? Zach typed in another command to show him everything that the system was doing. There was only one thing going on, and that thing confirmed his worst fears. The intruder was into the source files. . . the actual programs! What could he be doing? Zach wasn't sure what to do, the guy could be stealing the programs or even worse, changing them. His mind raced, looking for a solution. *'I'll just take the son of a bitch out.'* He had the power to do that. His hands trembled slightly as he reached out to the keyboard again. He typed in a command which closed down the outside phone lines, but then stopped midstream. *'Wait a minute,'* he told himself. *'If I do this, he can get right back in some other night. We need to know who it is and what he's doing.'* He couldn't waste any time and backspaced the keystrokes to erase that line and typed the command from a moment ago. Okay, the intruder was still there. Then Zach finally realized what he could do. As long as there was activity. . .the intruder kept working on the programs, he could have the phone company trace it down to its origin. He grabbed the phone at the far end of the table and brought the receiver up to his ear.

"Freeze, right there!" a voice yelled.

The receiver hit the floor with a loud thud. Zach spun instinctively around and then froze as the voice had commanded. He was staring straight down the barrel of a .357 magnum revolver. The hammer was cocked! On the other side of the gun was a very large intimidating silhouette illuminated by the hallway light with the computer room door standing wide open now. The silhouette reached to the wall and flipped the light switch without budging the gun in the other hand. Zach squinted his eyes for a second before he could see the man. In front of him, stood a very rough looking middle-aged man with a small pot belly. His hair was dark and greased back, like the fifties look. From the look of his face, Zachery knew that he meant business. The man seemed to come from nowhere. Zach glanced at the camera in the corner, wondering if it had given him away. Well, were the cameras real after all? No. Probably not. Maybe the guard had just heard noise from behind the computer room's double doors. As immersed in the computer as he was, the guard might have just walked in while making rounds. He decided to play it cool.

"Oh God, man, you scared the shit out of me! My name's Zach Crawford. I work here during the day." Zach slowly reached his hand out to shake the man's hand as he continued. "Are you a new security guard here?" The man was not receptive to his gestures and raised the gun higher in emphasis of his last statement.

Zach raised his hands back up slightly, hoping to show the gunman he wanted no conflict. He would try to reason with the man. "Hey, really, I work here. There's an unauthorized user on the computer system. I need to call the phone company so they can trace it."

Then the man yelled at Zach, "Touch that phone, and I'll blow your goddamn head off!"

Zach believed him, but he knew he had to do something about the intruder.

"Look," Zach said desperately. "Why don't you call someone? They'll verify who I am. I work for John Berringer, call him!"

He looked over his shoulder to the lights on the disk drives, which were still active. *'Shit,'* he thought to himself.

After a long silence, the man pulled a two–way radio from the back pocket of his dark blue uniform pants.

"Hey, Jim," he said, bringing it to his mouth while his eyes were still trained down the gun barrel to Zach's chest. "I got someone up here in the computer room, claims he works here, works for John Berringer. Do you have that name in the register?"

"Yeah," a voice came through the radio after a minute. "I got the name here."

"I'm gonna call him to verify his story."

"Come on," Zach refuted. "I didn't make it up."

The guard glared at Zach for this discretion and said, "You'd better be telling the truth or you're going to jail for a long time."

Not taking the gun sights off of Zach, the man walked over to another phone and picked it up with his free hand, dialing John's home phone number. Meanwhile, Zach continued to watch the gun, the intruder and then the gun again.

"Uh, Mr. Berringer sir, this is Wayne Cavanaugh. I've caught some guy up here sniffing around in the computer room. . . says he works here. He says his name is Zachery Crawford."

Zach watched and waited anxiously. Then the man took the phone away from his ear and held it straight out to Zach.

"Says he wants to talk to you," Cavanaugh said as he gave Zach a threatening look and handed him the phone.

Zach took it very slowly from the guard, who had at least started to lower the gun, however slightly.

"John!"

"Zach, is that you? What in blazes are you doing there so late?"

"John," he repeated. "Never mind that, tell this guy who I am. We've got a big problem here. Someone has broken into the system, they're using it right this minute!" The phone was silent. "John, did you hear me?" Zach was practically screaming.

"Uh, yeah. Sorry, I'm just surprised, shocked."

"I'm gonna run a trace on the phone line if this guy will let me."

"Okay, Zach. . . good idea. I'll be there in a few minutes. Let me talk to the guard again." Zach reached the phone back to the guard who moved in slow motion, obviously hoping to provoke Zach, who was still very anxious. He hung up the phone after a word with John and stood for what seemed an eternity to Zach. Finally, he holstered the gun and stepped back. The hate was still in his eyes, but Zach couldn't be concerned with that now. He lunged forward, grabbing the phone and dialing as fast as he could.

"C'mon, c'mon, answer damn it!" Finally, someone answered. "Yeah, this is Zachery Crawford with Global Computer. I've got an unauthorized user on our computer system. I need a trace run on it to see where it's coming from."

The voice on the other end was that of an older lady, "Is this some sort of joke?"

"This is not a joke." He repeated his name again. What was going on? The lady didn't say anything. That was it, his blood was boiling. Finally he exploded and screamed at the top of his lungs, "Look Bitch, if you don't run the goddamn trace right now, I'm gonna rip these lines out and shove them straight up your ass. Now, do it!"

"You realize sir, that we will have to charge for this, don't you?" she smarted off to him.

"I don't give a damn, just run it now!"

"Are you in a position to authorize such a charge, sir?" she provoked him further.

"Yes goddamn it! Are you in a position to lose your job?"

The guard took another step back, the look in his face changing from hate to almost fear. He wondered if Zachery was insane. Zach recited a circuit identification number of the phone line from his memory to the lady on the phone. Then he gave her his phone number, instructing her to call back as soon as she had the location. He slammed the phone down.

"Goddamn that bitch," he mumbled under his breath. Then something caught his eye. He leaned closer to the screen to read. The system was working a bit heavier now, which probably meant one thing. . .it meant the son of a bitch was getting out. He was probably saving everything right this minute so that he could get out.

"Damn!" Zach pounded his fist against the table, then looked over at the telephone. "Call, bitch, call."

He wanted to do something. He could stop the program to buy a little time, but if the intruder realized that it was taking too long, it wouldn't stop him from panicking and detaching from the line. There was no choice, Zach typed in a command to temporarily stop it. Now, he would just wait and hope that a trace was run before the intruder realized someone was onto him. Zach's eyes darted back and forth from the screen to the seconds ticking away on his watch. Thirty seconds. . .Forty-five seconds. . .Then it happened. Two harsh words appeared on the screen. . .Station Detached. Zach buried his head in his open hands and breathed deeply, trying to lower his boiling blood pressure.

After a moment the phone rang. Zach grabbed it, still clinging to a glimmer of hope.

"This is the phone company. Sir, our trace verified activity on the line, but the connection was cut before we could find the point of origin."

Zach slammed the phone down without saying a word. He slumped down into a chair, giving a loud sigh. The guard stood at the doorway, a bit apprehensive after the display he had just witnessed.

"Any sign of Berringer?" he mumbled into the radio.

"Yeah," the unseen voice replied. "I see his car pulling into the lot now. He'll be up in a minute."

John calmly entered the computer room, motioning for the security guard to leave. As he came closer, he asked Zach what was going on.

"I don't know where to start," Zach said throwing his arms into the air before explaining the entire event to John in full detail.

After he finished John asked, without raising his head, "So, you didn't get a location from the trace?"

"No, I'm sorry. The phone company didn't believe me at first. I had to argue with them before I could get them to start a trace."

"Okay, it's not your fault, Zach. I know you did what you could. Besides, it's probably just some kid snooping around."

Zach couldn't believe the lack of concern from John. "Come on, John, don't you think that we should call the police?"

John put his hand on Zach's shoulder and said, "Zach, it was probably nothing. We can check the files out tomorrow to make sure that everything's okay."

"But, John."

Zach was cut short. John's voice turned icy cold. He seemed to be trying to hold back his temper. "Have you thought of the publicity a police report like this would get us? We're supposed to be the best software house in the country, and if we can't write a goddamn security program to keep hackers out of our own system, why would anyone want us to write one for them? Do you know what that could do to our credibility?"

"Yeah, I know John, but I still think. . . "

He was again interrupted by John's stern voice, "Zach, we do not need to file a report, and that's final."

"Okay, okay," Zach finally agreed, "I guess that would look pretty bad. I'll just load in yesterday's back up tapes and check them for any prior break ins." Even as he made the statement, Zach wondered exactly how he might accomplish that.

"Why don't you go home and get some rest?" John said. "You look like you need it, and you're probably going to have a long day tomorrow, with trying to check these files out." His voice had returned to normal.

"Good night, John."

"Oh, Zach, did you see the paper?" John had a grin across his face as he changed the subject.

Zach looked at him, puzzled at first, before realizing John meant the article he had read about himself that morning. "Oh, yeah. I saw it."

"Congratulations, Zach."

"Thanks, John. That was nice of you."

"Well, you're welcome. You go on home now. I'll take care of locking things up here."

At that, Zach left. John walked to the window and pulled the curtains aside, watching the parking lot until he saw Zach walking towards his car. He leaned back a little bit as if trying not to be seen. As soon as Zach was gone, John went after the guard.

"Cavanaugh, from now on no one is to be in this computer room when you get here. Your shift is late enough that everyone should already be gone," he said forcefully.

Cavanaugh stood like a private at attention. "Yes, sir. I understand."

John continued, "If anyone's in here, then escort them out of the building immediately. I'm going home now, you close this place up." He turned and stepped into the elevator. Then with one last point of emphasis, he turned back and declared, "Cavanaugh, I mean no one."

The elevator doors slid shut.

Zach was exhausted and went straight to bed when he got back to his apartment. But he couldn't fall asleep. He was too wired to calm down. He lay in bed for several hours playing the scene over and over in his mind. He just couldn't understand how John could've been so calm. Things just weren't right there. Why didn't John seem to care? That system had information on huge department stores, financial institutions, even government military projects that Global did. . . Was there something wrong with John, was he in trouble or something? The thoughts raced back and forth. He just couldn't believe John could be doing something wrong, he had known him for too long. . . Maybe he was just concerned about protecting Global's reputation, like he said. After all, an incident like this could seriously hurt the company. There was no telling what new customers would do, the government, the company's stock price. John was right, it could be devastating. Even with the weight of all his problems, the fatigue did Zach in, and he finally dozed off.

Chapter
Eight

Once again Zach had to drag himself out of bed the next morning. As he dressed for work, his mind was already racing with the events from the night before. He had only been able to sleep two or three hours and was very tired, but at least he wasn't plagued with the dream. Zach was not the type to miss work though. Global was good to him, so he had always given them everything it took. He was running late this morning so he skipped breakfast and grabbed his stuff, slamming the door to his apartment behind him.

The elevator took him down to the basement garage where the tenants parked their cars. It is said to be inconvenient to own a car in this town. The tenants of this building all had cars though. If you lived here, you had the money to overlook the problems of parking, insurance, etc. The elevator slowly came to a stop and doors slid open. A cold breeze swept in through the doors and caught Zach by surprise, sending a chill up his back. He shook it off, stepped from the elevator and started to his car.

Then he stopped suddenly. *'What was that?'* he said, almost aloud. A quick low shuffling noise had come from only a few cars away. The basement was dark though, and the noise echoed out of every corner, even though it was faintly more than a whisper of sound. He wheeled about in a complete circle looking for the source of the noise. . . Nothing. *'Where was the night watchman?'* he wondered. He was usually in sight somewhere in the garage, since it wasn't very big. He stood still for a moment, continuing to search, but the guard was nowhere in sight and it was silent again. Suddenly, a roar seemed to burst out of the silence. Zach's heart jumped up in his throat. He spun wildly around, his arms flailing from centrifugal force. The source of noise was right behind him. It was only the elevator door, faithfully performing its mundane job. Zach exhaled a small sigh of relief at the sight. An older woman stepped into the basement barely taking notice of him as she strutted over to a nearby Mercedes. She lived a few floors below his apartment if he recalled properly. His attention turned back away from the snooty old bitch. Maybe the shuffling noise was just an animal or something. With the events of the previous evening, Zach figured that he was just imagining things, shrugged it off and went on to his car.

The day turned out to be slow and calm, unlike the day before. However, Zach wasn't getting any work done on the LakeShore project. Instead, he was busy worrying about John and the intrusion into the system. . .. He couldn't help but wonder if something internal was wrong. He sat alone in his office staring at the closed door while repeatedly entwining two paper clips together like a chain, then taking them back loose again. He just couldn't concentrate.

A knock at the door startled Zach out of his deep thought. Two gentlemen entered. They were the same two who had had the problem in the computer room, Cowboy Bob and his trusty sidekick, Jerry.

"What do you have for me?" Zach asked them as they walked across to his desk.

"Nothing," they both shrugged. "Everything looks good; no signs of any tampering or viruses or. . ."

Their voices trailed off as a look of disgust enveloped the face of their boss.

"Did you check sizes and access dates on the file listings?"

"Yeah," Cowboy answered shaking his head.

"What about the automatic system logs?"

Both shook their heads again in confirmation.

"Come on!" Zach was trying to hold back, but his frustration found its way out. "You guys can't find anything? Something should show on the logs. He was there, I saw it myself. I know the guy was doing something. . .And you guys come in here and tell me you can't find shit! What is your problem? You should be smarter than some damn stranger off the street."

"Get off it, Zach!" Bob jumped back. "This system is huge. It's hard to find anything in it. . .no less a fuckin' needle in a haystack like this!"

Zach glared into his eyes a moment and lowered his head. One thing he always believed in was speaking your piece, standing up for yourself. He always conveyed this to his employees. They were never to back away from a confrontation with him just because he was the boss. Zach felt that this approach allowed them to work closer and more efficiently without the delays and misunderstandings of miscommunication, no trips to Abilene.

"Okay, okay," he retreated while raising his head. "You're right, I know. It's just that we need to find out what the hell's going on here. I didn't mean to jump down your throats."

"We're doing all we can."

"I know you are, Bob. Keep it up. . .Let me know if you find anything."

They turned and left the room.

His programmers had checked out everything and said it looked okay, but he couldn't believe that no changes had been made. It would be easy to hide things in a large system, a system such as this. A changed version of a program could be saved under a completely unrelated name, with no hint at what it really was, then switched out later for the good copy and quite possibly never be caught.

What would the motive be for such an act? To insert a menacing virus maybe. . .Or to steal the code, or data? His guys obviously didn't realize how concerned he was. They hadn't found any trace.

But on the other hand, maybe it was up to him. After all, he knew this system better than anyone, including them. He could set traps to tell him when someone had been snooping around, to tell him when they went into the system, when they went out of the system and to tell him what they did to the system.

Should he do such a thing? He really didn't have the time. Maybe it was a one time shot. . .and wouldn't happen again. But he couldn't take that chance. He felt responsible. He knew what happened. It was his security system that had been broken, and John had pointed it out last night, rather indirectly, but Zach caught the accusation just the same. He owed John and this company an answer.

Across the hall, John's office was empty. He had taken the elevator up to the seventh floor. It was only one flight up, but it was a place that the average Global employee would never see. The shiny chrome-like elevator doors slid open, revealing a world as different as day is from night. John stepped onto a very thick and plush tan carpet which spanned the entire lounge and hallways. Global's corporate emblem was inset in the middle of the lounge floor. It wasn't that the offices downstairs were bad, just that the ones up here were magnificent. The whole place reeked of money.

John walked across the lounge, unaffected by the lavish surroundings. It was decorated with elegant wallpaper and Queen Anne style furnishings with a large, glass chandelier centered on the ceiling.

"Good afternoon, Mr. Berringer. I'll tell him you're here." The voice was that of the beautiful brunette receptionist across the lounge.

"All right, thank you, Cindy," John acknowledged. He watched as she picked up the phone and informed her boss of his arrival. After hanging up the phone, she looked back at John and motioned. "He said to go right in."

"Thank you."

John walked down the empty hallway. It was nothing like the other floors crowded with people rushing back and forth and in and out. Up here it was a calm atmosphere. There were no busy workers running back and forth, because this was top management. The company was run from here, like the bridge of a battleship with commands given out to the crew below. John walked up to the only set of doors on the right side of the hallway. He knocked politely and waited a moment before entering 'HIS' office.

He was James Richard VonEric, the most powerful man at Global. VonEric had been CEO and President for most of the years since John was first hired as a young and ambitious programmer, much like Zach. John took a glance around the office even though he was familiar with it. It was huge, even in comparison to John's. There were several rooms. The main one, the office itself, which John had just entered was very large and had a 10' ceiling. A dark mahogany wood desk acted as the centerpiece of the room, with matching bookcases to each side. John scanned the bookcases, which contained many business related publications as well as a collection of classics. Interestingly, most were of a macabre variety, Edgar Allen Poe, Bram Stoker and Dante. Several doors opened to other unknown rooms.

James VonEric was leaning against the front of his desk, facing the door as John walked in. He was a tall overpowering man with coal black hair receding on his smooth sloping forehead. His face was rough, but clean-shaven, and he had small, cold, icy blue eyes. He looked like the absolute model of a corporate business professional. His body was lean and trim, and he wore a custom tailored dark blue suit. Upon John's arrival, he stood up and uncrossed his arms. He stood in front of John, a pillar of power, his very presence seemed to permeate the room.

"Good afternoon, John."

"How are you, James?" John replied.

VonEric walked across the room to a small bar at the bookshelves.

"Would you like some cognac?" he asked John holding up a partially filled crystal carafe.

"No, I'm fine."

"John," VonEric's eyes seemed to turn even icier as he peered at John through the tiny slits. "What is this I hear about Zach Crawford last night?"

"Well, James," John began. "He was here working late last night, and on his way out he noticed that someone was using our computer system. He didn't get a trace or anything, but he's very concerned about it."

"Do you expect any trouble out of him?" asked VonEric.

"I don't think so. I'm sure I can smooth it over."

"You better be sure of it." VonEric paused in thought. "Just the same, I want his home phone bugged."

"It has already been taken care of." Then John continued. "We always monitor key personnel during these projects. He's never been a problem on any other projects. But he's matured a lot since he came to the company, and he's very ambitious. Not to mention, he's quite a brilliant technical mind."

"So, in your opinion, John, he doesn't know anything?"

"Oh no sir, I'm sure that he didn't find out anything last night."

"All right, John, keep him under close surveillance, and if he's up to something, I expect you to act appropriately. Judging from your description of this Crawford, he won't just drop this thing."

"I'll watch him. . .make sure he drops it," John assured him obediently.

VonEric walked around to the back of his desk, sat down and began reading over some correspondence. John watched him silently for a minute before he looked back up.

"That will be all, John. Keep me posted."

"Yes sir." Without another word, John silently exited the room.

Back on the sixth floor, John walked through the computer room toward the opposite hallway. The men and women he passed spoke dutifully and smiled. They didn't know the thoughts that occupied his head now, nor would they ever. He just smiled back, asking of family members, work projects, etc., the same thing he always did. He was John Berringer, their compassionate employer.

His cold hand opened the door, and he walked down the hallway that housed both his and Zachery's offices. The doors faced off directly in front of him. His eyes rolled left to his office then back right to Zach's newly acquired one. Suddenly, in a burst, he reached to the right and swung open that door.

Zach, his back turned, swung around in the chair behind the desk.

"You surprised me, John," Zach said unsteadily. He reached his arm around and blanked out the terminal screen sitting on the credenza with one keystroke. "What's up?"

"Not much," John answered, glancing toward the terminal. "I just wanted to check and see how you were. . .you know, after last night."

Zach rose from his seat and made his way around the desk to John.

"To tell you the truth, John, not very good," he answered.

"What's wrong?" John's face showed concern.

"We just can't forget something like a break-in, John. I mean if someone were caught, actually in the building, they would be arrested and charged."

"That's just it, Zach," John justified. "It was a computer break-in, not a physical break-in."

"There's no difference!" Zach interrupted.

"There is a difference though. The public would perceive a computer break-in as negligence on our part."

"You mean 'shareholders' not 'public'!"

"Yes. Damn it, Zach, they own this company. They own you, and they own me."

"That's why I have to do something about it, John."

"Like what?" John tried to hide the concern from his face. He knew how smart Zach was. He had to be careful.

Zach looked down, wondering still how much he should do and how much he should say. He owed John a lot. John had always taken care of him. He trusted him, didn't he?

"I thought I would rework the security system. If I can figure out the breach, I can redesign it. . .and make it more difficult to break. I guess no system is infallible." Zach's words trailed off.

John treaded lightly. "Do you have the time right now, son? I can't afford for this bank project to get sidetracked and off schedule."

"Not really, John, but, I don't think we can take the chance of any more break-ins."

John could see that Zach wasn't giving up, just as he would have guessed.

"Well. . .okay. But I want to have complete details of any changes you make to security. Got it?"

Zach nodded. For some reason he had only mentioned the security system. He did intend to change security if he found a problem. But he hadn't mentioned the remainder of his plans. He didn't mention setting traps or catching the violator if he broke back in. For whatever reason, Zach had omitted this detail, deciding to hold his hand a little closer.

"By the way, John, has my clearance been changed?" Suddenly Zach wanted an answer to this question that he'd previously dismissed.

"Should've been increased. . .like we discussed," John answered. "Why?"

"I couldn't get in the computer room the other night. It was after 5:00, but my clearance has always been higher than that." Zach waited for John's reaction.

"It must be some mistake. . .Maybe when you were promoted, the security wasn't updated properly." John grinned. "I'll take care of it myself Zach, don't worry."

Zach followed him to the door and locked it behind him. He decided not to tell anyone of his plans. After all, there may be an insider. Maybe one of his team, like Roger or Bob, maybe even John? Zach thought of his remark to his men. "You should be smarter than a stranger off the street!" Yes, maybe they were smarter. Maybe one of them was behind this. Outsider or insider, he had to know what was going on.

He spent the whole afternoon setting his traps. The security system looked fine, so he did nothing to it for now. But in the system administration he made extensive modifications, adding hidden sub-routines to the communications programs and enhancing the system log routines. All changes were designed in the hopes of not being detected, such as making up common names for new routines and hiding them in the normal processes. The system log would now show entries from the violator and hide them so as not to be erased. If it happened again, the date, time and activity would be reported. Everything would be well documented. Zach Crawford was going to nail this bastard to the wall!

Chapter Nine

The time was 5:15, and Zachery knew that he had to leave early in order to make sure that he raised no suspicions. He wasn't sure what he wanted to do if he found something wrong, but it seemed only logical to start searching, and then cross those roads when he came to them. He had set up the system to keep track of anybody logged in between five o'clock in the evening and eight in the morning. Now he would just have to be patient and wait to see if the system was broken into again. While he hadn't changed the security system itself, the passwords were all updated. If someone was back in right away, then he had to have help from inside the company. Zach had confidence in the security system he had designed. He didn't believe that just anyone could get in whenever they wanted, no matter what John had insinuated. Now it was a waiting game. He'd just have to see what turned up Monday morning, if anything. Besides, he had better things to think about this weekend. Tonight was his date with Taylor.

Zach planned a nice, cozy, private dinner for two at a small steakhouse he knew of, and maybe some dancing afterwards to some slow jazz. He desperately hoped this would interest her. After all, he knew so little about Ms. Williams' likes and dislikes that he would just have to play it by ear and see how the evening turned out. His stomach was rolling with jitters, like a school boy. Obviously it had been way too long since he had been out with a woman. Concerns about dating his fellow employee still danced around in his mind, but he was now rationalizing it to himself instead of the reverse. After all, how could they deny the attraction they both felt.

He followed the instructions she had given him to her apartment. She lived in a very nice building, just a little north and west of the town. It was an older building with a recent facelift. There were twin atrium doors leading into the building. Zachery tried them, found they were locked and used the intercom on a side wall.

"Yes, hello?" It was Taylor responding.

"Taylor, this is Zach. . .Zachery."

"Oh hi, come on up. Just come on in when you get up here. It's on the third floor just to your left."

The entrance doors buzzed, allowing him to enter. Upstairs he knocked politely on her door, took a deep breath and walked in.

Upon hearing him open and close the door, Taylor yelled from a back room, "I'll be just a minute, you can fix yourself a drink if you like. It's on the dry sink in the living room to your right."

"Thank you," he yelled back, "you know you shouldn't leave your door unlocked. You never know what kind of wacko might walk in. I mean. . .look at me for instance."

She giggled lightly, still unseen to him. "Now, I just unlocked it when you buzzed." There was a short pause, "After all, I couldn't answer the door while I'm still undressed, could I?"

Zach was sipping the bourbon and soda he'd just finished mixing and almost choked. "Oh, I wouldn't have minded."

She giggled again, only this time louder. He turned around and saw her standing in the hallway.

"You look great!" he said with his eyes looking up and down her body. She was wearing a royal blue dress, cut into a deep plunging v-shape in both the front and back. It fit tight against her magnificent body, hugging every wonderful curve, and a length short enough to immediately draw his attention to her dark shapely legs. Her hair flowed evenly, resting on both shoulders.

"Why, thank you. So do you."

Zachery took several steps in her direction. Being a little closer, he marveled at how the dress pulled the rich blue from her beautiful eyes.

On the way to the restaurant, neither said much. Both worried about how their business relationship would fare if their personal relationship grew stronger. This was it. It wasn't just the forbidden taboo here. The excitement was tantalizing, while absolutely frightening at the same time.

They drove down Lake Street, under the elevated train system, until they were close to the loop. Zach parked his BMW and ran around to get the door for Taylor. The restaurant was downtown, but secluded on a side road to itself.

"Here we are," Zach said pointing down a flight of stairs, leading into the basement of a building.

Taylor said nothing, trying to hide her reservations about the appearance of the entrance. Zach picked up on it right away though, probably expecting it.

"You've gotta give it a shot," he explained. "I know it doesn't look like much, but they have the best steaks in town." He put his arm around her waist and led her down the steps. It was the first real contact between them. She felt good close to him.

It looked somewhat nicer on the inside than on the outside. A very distinguished older gentleman greeted them and led them to a private booth in the back. The place looked more like an old small town tavern than a big city restaurant. The floors were bare stained wood, uncarpeted and worn along the pathways. There were several tables scattered in the middle of the room, with the booths wrapped around the walls. All the tables were lit by miniature brass gas lanterns, which provided the only light throughout the room. Taylor thought of old black and white gangster movies. This looked like the kind of place they used to hang out in. The entire restaurant must have seated only thirty people.

It was starting to grow on her, as she and Zachery shared a carafe of red wine. With plants dangling all around, a very intimate atmosphere had been created. They made small talk for awhile, then Zach ventured into a more meaningful conversation, which dwindled through dinner and dessert.

"Well," Zach said, placing his napkin on the table and sipping his coffee. "Was this a good choice?"

"Very good."

Zachery gazed across the table at her. The dim light seemed to make her even more gorgeous. He wasn't sure how that could be, she was already more beautiful than any girl he'd ever seen. He watched the light glistening and sparkling through the sandy waves in her hair.

"You know, I meant what I said earlier," he said.

She looked back at him a bit puzzled, "What?"

"You do look great," he said repeating his earlier statement as he reached across the table taking her hand into his. He prayed that she didn't find this trite. "As a matter of fact, you are a gorgeous woman, Taylor Williams."

"Thank you," she said softly. She wasn't the type of woman to be embarrassed by a compliment, but her thanks were sincere. She put her other hand on top of his on the table, so that now all four were joined.

She was looking back into his eyes and thinking the exact same thing. *'You're gorgeous.'* He was a complex man, this Zachery Crawford. He was ruggedly handsome, yet so mature and sophisticated. His masculine physique showed his determination to be a real man's man, but his mannerisms could be so gentle and sensitive. At work, he was the pillar of success and confidence, with almost an arrogance about him. Yet in person he seemed so down to earth, so thoughtful. It seemed to her that it was what true confidence did for a man, giving him the comfort to be himself. . .in any situation. She watched as he signed for the check, wondering how it might feel to run her fingers through his wavy hair. . .across his bare chest.

"Taylor." Zach paused and smiled. "Thank you very much for tonight."

"You're welcome, Mr. Crawford," she said after a pause. She had hoped to spend more time with him.

"I've had a great time. It's been a long time since I've been out with anyone. . .and it was worth the wait."

"Thank you, too, Zachery. I had a good time. Dinner was excellent, and so was the company."

"But you were worried, huh?" Zach motioned to indicate that he was speaking of the restaurant.

"Okay. Yes, I was worried!"

"Are you ready to go?"

"Sure, anytime you are," she answered softly.

They walked slowly to his car with their arms wrapped around each other. It was a welcome feeling for both of them, this closeness. As they came to the car, Taylor seemed to take notice of the canvas soft top.

"Zach, can we put the top down?"

"Don't you think that it's a little bit cool?"

"Yeah, but it feels good," she leaned up to his ear and whispered softly. "Please?"

Zach grinned from ear to ear, shaking his head. "Yeah, you know when you've found a sucker, don't you?"

She just laughed and stepped into the car. His eyes were riveted to her legs as she slid one into the car, and slowly crossed them. The short blue dress rode up very high on her thighs. With exacting purpose, she tugged it back down, but only an inch or so, luring his starry gaze. Partially regaining his composure, Zach shut her door and bounced around to the driver's side.

"Are you tired?" He prayed that she answered no.

"Not really. What did you have in mind?"

"Good," he sighed with relief. He desperately wanted to continue the evening. "Do you like to dance?"

"I love dancing."

"I know this quiet little place we could go to. The band plays this soft mellow jazz that you could dance to all night."

"That sounds nice," she answered, with a subtle sexiness to her voice. Silently Taylor was cheering, as happy as Zach that the evening wasn't over.

"Good."

'Boy, you really know how to turn a guy on, Taylor,' he thought to himself. Here was a powerful young man who was successful at everything he did. He dealt with powerful people all the time, people that would try to influence him and win him over, manipulate him any way they could. He'd always had a sense with that.

And he certainly wasn't inexperienced with women. He had dated plenty long enough to see many types of women. From dumb ignorant girls to devious troublesome vixens, he'd seen his share of all. Now here he was, and Taylor had him wrapped around her finger using only simple, playful flirtation. He couldn't imagine what might happen if she turned it up a notch.

They drove along the lake shore, catching the cool brisk wind blowing off Lake Michigan. The city was lit up by millions of lights. Closer into downtown, it was nearly like day, with thousands of cars still bustling through the busy streets. Taylor slid toward the middle and leaned her head against Zachery's shoulder, and he held her close. He wondered if his life had been slipping away over the years. Had too much emphasis been placed on his career. . .at the expense of his happiness?

After about a twenty–minute drive, Zach turned onto a side road. *'Another dive,'* Taylor thought to herself, but entrusted him anyway. *'He had been right the first time, so, reserve judgment,'* she told herself.

Inside, the club was very dark. Only a single dim light shone over the band and then a few neon signs about on the walls. The place was very crowded, and the dance floor jammed. They sat, but only for a short time.

"Would you care to dance?" Zach asked her.

"I would," she answered. "Are you sure you want to?"

"I'm positive," he responded somewhat confused.

"It's just that a lot of men don't like to dance," she explained.

"What man would turn down a chance to hold you in his arms," Zach whispered slyly.

He led her slowly through the darkness to a small opening on the dance floor. They turned to each other, Zach wrapping his arms around her waist and Taylor reaching over his broad shoulders, clasping her hands behind his neck. She liked the feeling of his large powerful hands in the small of her back, pulling her tight against him. She rested her head against his solid chest where his heart beat strongly in her ear. Her fingers explored, moving slowly over his chest, over the rounded muscles in his wide shoulders and clasping back together around his warm neck.

Zach pulled her closer still. The sweet fragrance of perfume radiated from Taylor up to his nose. He touched his cheek to her soft wavy hair, and his controlling hands slid up and down her spine so gently, yet so longingly. He felt flushed as he thought of her body against his, her breasts pushed firmly against his chest. His mind fantasized of the two of them alone, dancing in the nude. . .her chest against his. . .grasping her firm round ass with both his hands. . .then falling to the floor and making love for hours.

Their heads parted. They gazed into each other's eyes for seemingly an eternity, swaying to the music still. Finally, Zachery lowered his head and their lips met. His hand pulled her face tight against his. It was a timid kiss at first, but quickly their tongues met in hungry exploration.

They danced for hours, relishing the closeness, the soothing tranquility, before the club closed in the early morning hours and ended their enchanted evening.

It was tough for Zach to end the evening as he walked Taylor to her apartment. They kissed yet again before she stepped through the door. She pulled it part way closed and leaned out the open space.

He wanted to ask her to let him in. She had not offered though, and he felt it might offend her.

"Taylor." Her name had come out before he could stop himself.

"Zach," she answered in barely more than a whisper. "I don't think it's a good idea, do you?"

"I don't know." His heart told him yes, while all forms of reason argued against it.

"Let's take it slowly, okay? We both need to consider what we're about to do." She paused as her hand touched his cheek. "I'd love to invite you in, but I don't think so. . .not yet, not tonight. Do you understand?"

"I understand."

"Do you?"

"Yes, I do understand," Zach reassured. And before she could reconsider, he kissed her goodnight and walked away.

Chapter Ten

Zach was undeniably infatuated with Taylor. He couldn't stay away. They went out again the next night. He couldn't resist calling her, even though they had been together less than 24 hours before. He hoped not to seem too anxious but had to take that risk. He couldn't bear to spend the night in his apartment with only his old friend, loneliness, to keep him company.

The call was no surprise as she had teased him about taking it slowly again before quickly giving him an answer of 'yes.' They played the game, but both knew the truth. She longed to be with him just as much as he with her.

Monday came. Zach was full of energy, wide awake and raring to go. As usual, he took the elevator to the garage. When the door opened, Zachery started to greet the watchman standing a few feet away, then realized it wasn't who he'd thought it was.

"Hi, how are you?" he asked.

The man turned and smiled at him, "Fine sir, how about yourself?"

The watchman was in his mid-thirties, kind of short and plump. His face was covered with a thick dark beard, and he wore a big grin across it. *'He looks like a jolly soul,'* Zach thought to himself.

"Fine, uh where's Paul?"

"Paul?" the man said with a puzzled look. "Who's Paul?"

"You know, Paul, the normal watchman?"

"Oh, I don't know. I put my application in here awhile back, and they just called me yesterday asking if I could come in. The guy on the shift before me said that the guy I'm replacing got his head bashed in." The man rambled on, rather oblivious to the subject of which he spoke. "Said he was here the other night when someone broke in, they busted him with a tire iron. He said the guy was in the hospital."

"Oh God, how serious is it? Do they know who did it?"

"I don't guess so," the watchman answered and continued his windy account. "The guy said that they found him between a few cars over on the far end of the lot there. They didn't find anyone else around. Strange thing is, they can't figure a motive. I mean his wallet wasn't stolen. None of the cars were broken into. . .Nothing!"

Zach felt a tingle of fear at the base of his spine as he listened to the man's story. He remembered that he hadn't seen Paul the other morning. It must have just happened when Zach came out. He remembered hearing something, too. The tingling grew and crept further up his spine until chill bumps rose on his arms.

"Well, when did they find him?" Zach asked.

"I guess around nine o'clock when the next shift came on. Supposedly the guy saw a stream of blood coming out from under a row of cars and traced it 'til he found the guy."

The same chill rose through Zachery again. *'That could have been me,'* he thought. *'That guy was in here when I was leaving.'* He tried to shake the chill, but only partially succeeded.

"God, that's terrible," he said back to the new watchman, his voice noticeably shaken.

"Yeah, there's a lot of crazies out there," he replied back. He didn't know the guy. . .so it wasn't any big concern of his. The jolly grin came across his face again. "Have a nice day, I'd better make the rounds now."

"Sure," Zach allowed. "Take it easy."

Zach caught up to Taylor in the parking lot at work and walked her in. The concerns about Paul quickly subsided as thoughts about Taylor replaced them. Already she seemed to live in his thoughts. They passed in the hall, and his eyes followed her. Across the large computer room, his attention was drawn to her like a magnet. He was so infatuated that he couldn't concentrate, couldn't even think of anything else.

And Taylor felt it, too. Her interest in Zach had grown. She longed to spend time with him. But she was new. She had not yet been accepted by her peers. How could she hope to be accepted if they all thought she was fucking him? He seemed to be so obvious. Taylor was getting confused, but she couldn't turn away from him though. It was just too strong.

They went out again the next evening, then again several days later. With each passing day, it grew stronger. She was so content while with him. But when they were apart, her concerns ran wild. The rest of Zach's employees weren't stupid. They had to have noticed by now. What could she do? What should she do?

◊   ◊   ◊

Work on the LakeShore project was picking up. They were several weeks into it, and Zach fought to concentrate so the project wouldn't fall behind schedule. He still had that knack for burying himself in work, but Taylor was always there. He knew they had to maintain the professionalism for both their sakes. His reputation depended on this, and her reputation would be built from it. She was good. She didn't need him professionally. She would excel anyway. Taylor was a strong, intelligent woman whom he could look up to and be proud of.

Zachery felt the other members of his team slowly accepting her. They saw the quality of her work, just as he did. But if they saw signs of their relationship, these feelings might be compromised. So he tried to bury himself in the day to day work and hide his feelings from the rest of the team.

So far the project was on schedule, a few minor setbacks here and there, but his team always took up the slack. Delivery on the equipment had been taken, and he was in constant contact with LakeShore and the team. Preliminary programming was still on schedule thanks to his talented people, and the database would be done by the end of the week. They worked better and closer than ever before. Zach was proud of them. The LakeShore project would be done on time, just as promised.

But one of these loyal talented employees of his may be a thief, a crook. Could they be? Which one could it be? Was it Cliff, timid little Cliff? He was a loner, an outcast. What about the two men who were searching the system for him, Bob and Jerry? What if it was one, or even both of them. Could he be so wrong about Bob? They could be mocking his futile efforts, enjoying the whole incident, laughing at the 'company man'. . . Big Zach Crawford, Global's own Clark Kent. It might explain why they found nothing. But, then again, he hadn't found anything himself either. That proves nothing. What about John? A friend and mentor through Zach's years at Global. Maybe it was none of them. Maybe no one was on the inside, just a snot nosed kid, hacking computers for a joy ride.

One thing was for sure, though. Something was going on. Zach had to figure it out. He had kept an eye on the traps. Sure enough, it had happened again. Zach had checked his logs a few times, and the intruder was back. The computer room console was the only place granted access to these files. He wasn't taking any chances. That way, the intruder couldn't get to them, only him. But every time he got close, an interruption stopped him. The computer room was a very busy place, and he couldn't afford to draw attention to himself, so he held back, still waiting for an opportunity to examine them more closely. All he could tell was that it was happening on a regular basis.

He debated about telling Taylor. But could she be involved? Ridiculous! She was the only one he really felt close enough to talk to. On the other hand, she shouldn't become involved. This was going to get tough. Zach felt it in his gut. When things got bad, Taylor wasn't going to be caught in the crossfire. He had to protect her. These thoughts tumbled endlessly through his mind every moment that he wasn't totally consumed. So he plowed ahead, trying to juggle it all.

"Zach?. . .Zachery?"

Taylor sat across from him, the candlelight flickering in her lovely eyes. He finally dug himself free of the thoughts to answer.

"Hmm. I'm sorry, what dear?" he finally responded.

"I said do you want a drink? The server is waiting."

"Oh yes," he turned his attention to the young gentleman at their side, who waited very impatiently. "I'll have a bourbon and seven. . .thanks."

The server nodded sarcastically and then scurried away toward the bar.

"What is wrong with you?" she questioned disgustedly.

Zach paused for a moment. Again he wavered. Should he tell her? It wasn't fair to treat her this way. This preoccupation might be interpreted as a lack of interest, and it most certainly was not. But once again Zach neglected to tell Taylor.

"I'm sorry," he answered. "There's a problem at work that's worrying me. It's not that important. Don't worry."

"Okay, whatever you say." She dropped it. . .again.

He sensed Taylor was dissatisfied with his answer.

"Now what's wrong with you?" Zach questioned coldly.

"Nothing Zach. . .Nothing at all," with extreme sarcasm.

"What is it?"

Taylor hesitated, but had to get it off her chest.

"Why won't you open up to me?" she demanded. "I spend every free moment with you. Can't you tell how much I care for you?"

Her eyes became watery as she fought back a flood of tears. He hadn't realized it was so obvious that something troubled him.

"I'm sorry, Taylor." He felt like a snail.

"I just don't understand you. You've got this shell around you. I'm allowed in, but only so far. . .and then you put this wall up. What's wrong with you? You have more than most people will in their entire life. I mean. . .what's the problem? Were you mistreated as a child? Do you have an ex-wife that broke your heart or something? I don't get it."

"I know, Taylor," he whispered, trying to absorb the jolt of her last comment.

"I care for you very much, Zach. I want to be there for you, whether it's good or bad."

"Okay. . .but please give me some time," he asked. "I've got to sort some things out. I just can't talk about it right now. But it's nothing to do with us. I'm happier now than I've been in years. You're great. I promise I'll tell you soon. Please though, don't give up on me." But Zachery still had no intention of telling her anything.

While not an explanation, this was a somewhat more acceptable answer. She told herself not to push. They had a good thing, and she could trust him, right? He had earned her trust and respect. He was different. He truly cared about her.

He took her hand, pulled it to his lips and kissed it.

With much effort, Zach pushed work from his mind. They talked through dinner, the conversation beginning to flow again. But it always did. Something about Taylor put Zach at ease. It was very therapeutic and seemed to be just the right medicine considering his recent developments.

As they left the restaurant, Zach turned to her and kissed her. They held each other tightly as the valet brought his car around. Zach was sure to get the door for her rather than the valet, who seemed quite disappointed, but grabbed a quick glance anyway as her legs slid into the seat. She reached her hand up to Zach's face and gently turned it until their eyes met.

"Zach, let's go to your place tonight."

This took Zach by complete surprise. To now, they'd followed their own advice, being careful and taking things slowly. He stared at her with a blank look on his face. After a moment, Taylor changed her expression, wondering, *'Did I say something wrong?'* But Zach quickly snapped out of it.

"Okay," he said trying to sound calm. "That sounds like a great idea."

Zach turned the car around and started back to his apartment, driving faster than normal, with his heartbeat about to match the rpm's of the car. He felt like a high school boy on his way up to Lover's Leap. It had been a long time since he'd made love to a woman. This wasn't about sex. It was much more than that. He actually felt himself growing nervous as they approached his house. The last woman he'd gone to bed with was wild, and in that case, getting laid was all that either of them was interested in. Oh. . .his lust for Taylor certainly ran deep, but this was special. Two people who cared for each other, sharing themselves, opening up to each other. The actual act of intercourse had been almost secondary. . .secondary to the expression of their true feelings for each other.

When they arrived, Zach unlocked the door to his castle, allowing Taylor to enter first. It was the first time she'd been to her man's home. She stood in the entrance way, looking down into the sunken living room and around the room. *'Very nice again, Crawford,'* she thought to herself. *'You don't disappoint, do you?'*

She felt Zach place his hands on her shoulders from behind, and ask, "Well, what do you think?"

"Very nice," she said with great emphasis, obviously approving of his taste in home decor.

"How 'bout a tour?"

"Yeah, I'd like that."

Zach led her through a quick tour, ending at the foot of his bed. Her eyes darted around the room, but were drawn to the bed over and over again. Not just yet though, as they moved to the balcony and shared a glass of white wine, enjoying the brilliant skyline.

With every second that passed, Zach wanted her more and more. The longing in his heart had become unbearable. He had to have Taylor. Standing behind her, his arms worked themselves tightly around her tiny waist. There was no denying themselves. Finally she spun to face him, and their lips met. Her tongue moved playfully just outside his mouth as Zach probed deeply with his. Their arms wrapped tightly around each other as a flood of emotion swept over them.

But then Zach retreated, realizing that soon there would be no turning back. He looked deep into her rich blue eyes for what seemed an eternity. What he felt could only be described as an insatiable craving, but he had to be sure. . .if only for her sake at this point.

"Taylor, are you sure this is what you want?" he asked. It could get very complicated from here forward, something they both were very sure of.

"Yes, Zach," Taylor answered softly.

"But, if we. . ."

"Zach," she interrupted, placing her finger to his lips. "Make love to me."

He moved slowly, savoring the intensity, as his hands ran through her soft wavy hair and across the soft contours of her face. Their tongues darted freely, exploring each others' mouths, as the pace quickened naturally. She wrapped her arms around him again, pulling him very close and tight to her.

Zach could feel the blood pulsing through his body, with hers against his, her breasts pushing against his chest.

He leaned back, sliding his hands down her neck and across her shoulders until they caught her dress and slid it over her shoulders. It seemed to float to the ground.

Taylor's blood was boiling as passionately as Zach's. She lifted her hands to the clasp on her skimpy bra. Her fingers released the bra hook where it sprung open in the front exposing her voluptuous breasts. The bra slid off her shoulders and to the floor with the dress. She gasped as the cool lake breeze hit her bare chest. Zach anxiously slid silk white panties over her hips where they joined the rest of her clothing in a pile at her feet. She stepped out of them, towards Zach, her head high and her eyes looking straight at him. Silently she offered herself to him.

He slowly looked her body up and down several times. It was bronzed evenly all over. Her breasts were firm and her nipples hard from the cool wind blowing across them. Beautiful curves and a flat stomach accentuated her athletic body. Taylor took great care of her body.

Her arms were at her sides, waiting for Zachery to take the lead. He slowly ran his hands down her sides and over her smooth hips, then swooped her up into his arms and carried her into the bedroom where he gently laid her onto his bed.

Taylor's heart fluttered at a lightning pace with the way that Zach held her, so strong, yet so gentle. She unbuttoned his shirt slowly, then tossed it aside to the floor exposing his muscular chest. She had longed to see it for so long it seemed. She let her hands brush across the muscles and hair but wanted more.

Zach stood beside the bed, sliding his slacks and briefs down, then stepped toward her slowly. Taylor's eyes explored his extraordinary frame freely as his eyes did hers. He, too, had a full tan, though not as dark. The biceps bulged in his arms while his shoulders were wide and rounded with muscle strands. Her hands returned to his chest, rubbing across the muscles and through the dark hair that tapered down his washboard stomach and beyond. Her eyes stayed fixed as she took him into her hands, massaging and watching him begin to grow.

His physique was breathtaking. He obviously took care of himself also, bridging that fine line between a sexy muscular frame, yet without the huge bulges of a bodybuilder.

He moved to her, taking her into his arms, feeling their naked bodies against each other for the first time. They kissed again, freely exploring each other with quick darting tongues.

Zach cupped his large hand over her breast, squeezing gently. It was firm, but yet so soft. Her breaths grew deeper as he excited her, and she closed her eyes, submitting to his total exploration of her body.

Every inch of her was incredibly sexy, everything about her turning him on. It had been so long since being with a woman. She drove him wild; he was so very excited. He wanted her more than any other woman he had ever dreamed of, and he couldn't wait any longer, finally entering her, their bodies tingling madly. Gone was the slow gentleness he had started with, their passions, instincts turning them into animals. They felt no inhibitions, no concerns, only the desire to express the feelings in the most intimate way possible. Finally they collapsed into each others' arms, totally fulfilled.

Exhaustion quickly set in as Taylor curled up, laying her head on Zach's chest. He wrapped his arms around her, pulling her tight, and they both slipped into a deep sleep.

Chapter Eleven

Four hours later, 5:00 A.M., and Taylor was lying awake in bed, unable to sleep. Well, it was done. They had crossed that line, and her mind raced in every direction.

She quietly got out of bed so that she didn't disturb her lover and went to the kitchen. The apartment was quiet and dark except for a very dim reflection of moonlight entering through the patio doors. It wasn't much light, but it was enough to guide Taylor through the unfamiliar surrounding as she poured a glass of water and moved to the living room couch to drink it.

She curled up, pulling her legs tight to her body and resting her chin on her knees. All she could think about was Zach Crawford, and these thoughts frightened her. A sensation of warmth came over her, just thinking of him. When they had made love several hours ago, it was the best she had felt in years. He was so good to her, always treating her like an intelligent person. . .not woman, but person. So many men just wanted sex, but Zach was different. They were lovers now, but they were also friends.

Then there was the thought that frightened her. . .she was falling in love with him. She told herself that it was too short a time, that she didn't know him that well. She told herself it could never work out. . .He was her boss for Christ's sake! All logical reasoning told her no. She kept coming up with the same conclusions time after time, though. She couldn't love him. She shouldn't love him. But she did love Zachery Crawford.

Something then broke into her thoughts. It was a noise emanating from the bedroom. She calmly walked to the doorway, expecting to find her lover awake, but this wasn't the case. The noise was in fact Zachery, but he was still sound asleep.

She moved closer to check on him. He was tossing back and forth in the bed, his whole body wringing wet with sweat. What should she do? Did he have a fever? Was he hallucinating?

She put her hands on his shoulders and gently shook him, unsure of whether to wake him or not. He didn't respond, so she shook a little harder as she was becoming somewhat frightened.

Zach jumped up suddenly, grabbing her shoulders tightly and gasping for air. His eyes were red, and his face glistened with sweat. He caught his breath for a moment, his senses returning and then realized it was Taylor. With that realization, he wrapped his arms around her like a small child looking for comfort.

"What's wrong, Zach?" she asked, terrified.

"Nothing. . .nothing," he answered hesitantly. "It was just a dream."

"You mean a nightmare!"

"Yeah, I guess you could call it that."

She looked him in the eyes. Here was a side to Zachery that she had never seen. A side that was frightened and vulnerable, a side that was like a child.

"Do you want to tell me about it?"

Zach shook his head no and sat up on the side of the bed, turning his face away from her. She knew that they didn't know each other that well, but this hurt anyway. A tightness quickly developed inside her. What she didn't know was that it hurt Zach also. For a split second he was considering telling her his dark secret. He quickly reconsidered, though. He'd never told anyone; he couldn't, not even Taylor.

"I thought maybe you had a fever or something, Zach."

"No! It's not a fever," he snapped back at her.

"Fine. . .no problem. I was just worried about you." Her voice was shaky as she tried to hide the pain that she was feeling. "I think I should go now," she said, scurrying for her clothes.

A sick feeling gnawed at his gut when he realized what he had done to her. Taylor had nothing to do with this. She had been nothing but wonderful and caring, and he was so busy feeling sorry for himself that he might as well have slapped her across the face.

"Taylor," he called, still looking in the other direction. He felt like a heel and didn't want to face her.

"What, Zach?" Her tone was harsh.

"Will you stay, please?"

It froze her in her tracks. She did want to stay, so desperately. She walked around the bed to look him eye to eye. "Do you really want me to?"

"Yes, very much," he answered softly. "I'm sorry I jumped down your throat. It has nothing to do with you, I know that. I'm just tired and grumpy."

"Okay, I'd like to stay," she said softly, running her fingers through his hair. "Can I get you some aspirin?"

Before Zach could answer, Taylor pulled open the drawer of the nightstand beside the his bed to search for it. She gasped lightly at the sight before her.

A small hand gun lay toward the back of the drawer, partially covered by some papers. It was a normal looking gun, a revolver, with a snub nose barrel. The blueing was dull in places, but the ".38 caliber" engraved in the side was still legible.

"What's wrong?" Zach asked after her gasp.

"It's the gun. . .I hate guns."

Zach hesitated for a moment then closed the drawer without touching the gun. It'd been a while since he'd thought about it being there.

"So do I," he explained to her.

"Then why do you have one?"

"I don't know," he stuttered. "I guess it's for protection."

"Zach, they're dangerous. You know the stories:

People getting shot with their own gun or accidentally shooting a friend or family member because they don't realize who it is and panic."

"Okay, okay," Zach interrupted harshly.

She hadn't expected him to snap at her so quickly. His emotions were all over the place. She considered leaving again, but it was obvious that Zach needed her. He was hurting and vulnerable right now. It was a side of him that surprised and to a degree, concerned her. But it was too late. She had already fallen so deeply for him that it would take wild horses to drag her away.

Taylor bit her tongue in an effort to avoid verbally retaliating. After a long pause, she decided to change the subject. He was obviously still shaken up from his nightmare.

"Look, the sun's coming up." She eyed the beginnings of light permeating out over the lake. "You know, I bet the sunrise looks great from here, let's go out and watch it. Then maybe I'll fix us some breakfast."

"Oh, you don't have to do that, Taylor."

"I know I don't have to," she said, grinning to him sarcastically, "I want to. So shut up and tell me, what you want."

"It doesn't matter, I've got bacon and eggs."

"That's fine."

"But I gotta warn you. . .I hate crispy bacon."

"What? You think I can't cook?"

"I don't know. Can you?"

"You better watch it jerk, or you'll get the crispiest bacon you ever saw. And, you'll like it."

He laughed at her as she gave him a disgusted look, smiled, then walked out of the room.

Zach turned to the nightstand where the gun was stored. He hated guns more than anyone. But that old .38 special was kept there. . .always. He hoped the subject didn't come up again as he looked away and met Taylor on the balcony.

Zachery and Taylor ended up spending the whole day together, which then turned into the whole weekend. Everything was so fresh. Their bodies tingled with energy. It seemed like the two of them were the only two people in the world. They did everything, and did nothing. All they needed was an excuse to be together, a little sight-seeing, a museum, movie, whatever. . .

Taylor was raised north of town in Wisconsin. After earning her bachelor's in California, she had returned to the area five years ago. Ever since that time, she had submersed herself in work, building a career without slowing down to enjoy life. It was easy enough for Zach to criticize, but how different was he, with it being over a year since he'd taken in the city.

With so many things to do, Chicago was a city that made it easy for young people to fall in love. That afternoon he took her to see the Cubs play, using a pair of Global's box seats from where the game was much more enjoyable. Naturally, she surprised him again. She was quite a fan. They jokingly argued about players' stats and the pros and cons of putting lights in at Wrigley Field.

After darkness fell, they went to the observation deck in the Sears Tower. It was a beautiful, cool spring night. The air still had the light crispness to it, not yet loaded down with summer smog. Lights from thousands of cars moved in and out of great highways, spanning out from the city in every direction. The moving lights looked like huge electronic blood vessels pumping life through the city, just as a huge heart.

Zach and Taylor roamed around arm in arm, playfully kissing each other. They were like new high school sweethearts out on a field trip together. The sight-seeing wasn't that important, most times not even really seeing the sights, but being together and learning each other.

The next day they wandered downtown shopping and then went to the Lincoln Park Zoo. It had been a long time since either of them had stopped long enough to enjoy the simple things so often overlooked. Now they enjoyed them together, gaining a new appreciation for these things as they saw them through each other's eyes. It was peaceful and relaxing for both, a change of pace away from their frantic, busy career schedules.

That night they played high school sweethearts again with the exception of their surroundings. Instead of a dark side road in the back seat of a car, they had Zach's lavish condo. As soon as they were inside the door, their arms were wrapped around each other, allowing their hungry tongues to meet in a passionate kiss. They peeled each others' clothes off and collapsed onto the living room floor together, making love.

Later in the evening, they shared a midnight snack and squeezed into a chair together to watch a late movie. Even the most average of happenings was so substantial, so rewarding. After the movie, Taylor led Zach back to the bedroom where they made love for hours, lasting into the early morning when they finally fell into a deep sleep with their naked bodies wrapped tightly together.

The weekend came to a close, and it was Monday morning, time to go back to work. But Zach and Taylor couldn't stand being apart. The days seemed to drag by as they longed to be in each others' arms. Their evenings were spent together, grasping every moment possible for each others' company. They really couldn't fight it any longer. In the short time that they had known each other, they had stopped denying their love.

While at the office, though, they were careful to conduct themselves professionally, at least in public. There were the playful looks in the hallway, the teasing letters carefully placed in desk drawers and even juicy private little conversations sent back and forth to each others' computer terminals. It was all so childish and frivolous, and so soothing to their hearts, especially Zach's burdened one.

And Zach had a schedule to keep. With nearly two months gone by in the project, they were still loosely on schedule. An application prototype was to be delivered by week end, and the problems with it seemed to be compounding hourly.

But more than anything else, he had the other worry. The intruder continued to dial in almost nightly as Zach checked the records from afar. He'd given the opposition some room to maneuver, and it appeared that it had worked. After nearly three weeks, they thought he had backed off and forgotten the whole thing. This person didn't know Zach Crawford, though. He didn't back down.

In a strange way it was exciting. It was him against them, cat and mouse. And it was up to each to outsmart the other one. What they didn't know was that Zach had a secret weapon hidden safely away, not up his sleeve, but in the depths of his computer.

This was by no means a game, though. What if these people were dangerous? He tried not to think of the possibility. Hopefully, when the person or persons responsible were discovered, they would confess quietly, and maybe the firm's reputation and personnel would be spared the public humiliation. There was no telling how many people and how much money might be involved. But weren't these things always about money? One thing was for sure though, there was something wrong, and he intended to find out what it was. Zach owed his firm this much.

Zachery thought back to his high school days when he first started driving a car. He remembered this friend of his who had built himself a muscle car. It was a 1969 Chevy Camaro Z28. They put a 396 c.i. big block in it, and it would scream. On the weekends they cruised town and looked up races. Then they'd go to this deserted road out in the country. It had corn fields lining both sides and was straight as far as the eye could see. All the hot shots went there to race. It always started off around twenty, maybe fifty bucks, but the stakes grew higher as the night grew later. That was a game that had to be played real cool. They would lay back several races to throw off the competition and just barely squeak out the win. When the stakes got high enough, they surprised everyone. The car was faster than anyone expected. Yeah, they always headed home with two or three hundred bucks after the big race.

'That's kind of what I'm doing now,' Zach thought to himself as he sat and stared at a blank computer screen. *'I'm hanging back this week, then come Monday I'll have the records I need to nail you.'*

Then his mind wandered back to another time from his high school days. A kid that no one knew from another school had worked his way in on the action. He drove a shitty looking Pontiac that looked like it was ready for pasture. Zach and his buddy had thrown a race or two while this out-of-towner had squeaked by a couple of guys in his junk heap. But when they lined up beside him for the big race, he was the one that had the surprise for them. He dusted them off like they were driving mommy's station wagon. They weren't even in the same league with the guy.

Zach shook his head strongly. He wouldn't let that happen here. He wasn't about to be outclassed. When it involved computers, particularly Global's computers, he prided himself on the extent of his technical abilities.

There was also another problem. . .the dreams. They had steadily been getting worse, not the dream itself. The dream was always the same, down to every last miserable detail. But it was happening more and more often. Zach couldn't understand why it came and went through the years. He would be fine for three, six, nine months, and then it would reappear for no apparent reason, only to haunt him again and eventually dissipate for another few months.

As if having the dreams weren't bad enough, Taylor had been pressuring Zach to tell her what was wrong. She had a very keen sense about her and realized for some time now that he was a troubled man. He could tell that he was hurting her by keeping silent, and the strain was beginning to show on their relationship. But he just couldn't bring himself to do it. He didn't know if he could ever tell anyone, no matter how much he cared for them. How could she have feelings for a man who had such a terrible secret in his past?

The weekend came, and Zach saw his prototype go out to the customer. It was only 80 percent but would still serve its purpose. He knew the team should work, if only to complete the prototype, but he offered movie passes and the weekend to all as a reward. And some selfishness had also played into his decision.

Saturday evening Zach and Taylor were lying side by side on the couch. The afternoon had been strangely quiet, and he couldn't help but feel that it was this wedge. . .being slowly driven between them by the dream. He hoped a day out in the sun would relax him. He'd always liked being outdoors. Maybe it would do him some good.

"What do you wanna do tomorrow?" he asked, leaning up to see her bright soothing eyes in front of him.

"I don't care," she answered.

"Well, I had this idea yesterday."

"What is it?"

"Well. . ."

"Come on, Crawford. Spit it out. I'm starting to get worried here."

"Okay. How would you like to go skiing tomorrow?"

"Skiing?" she said sounding surprised. "You mean water or snow skiing?"

Zachery laughed at her. "Water skiing. Where are we gonna find snow this time of year?"

"Well, Zach. I thought maybe you were talking about whisking me off my feet and flying me to Switzerland." She grinned at him teasingly as the worried look appeared on his face.

"We can do that next weekend." He paused for a moment and sarcastically grinned back at her. "This friend of mine has a boat on the Chain-O-Lakes. I called him up, and he said we could borrow it. Can you water–ski?"

"Just a little bit," she answered.

◊   ◊   ◊

In the morning they ran to her apartment so Taylor could find her bathing suit, which was still packed away. He paced around in the living room, patience dwindling, as he watched the bright sun rise higher into the sky.

"C'mon babe, we don't want to waste the day away," he yelled as he continued to look out the window. When it came to sports, he was still very much like a little kid. And though he tried not to rush her, he was very anxious to hit the water for the first time this season.

"I'm ready." Her voice carried a seductive tone.

When he turned around, his eyes bugged open wide. Taylor was standing in front of him wearing nothing but a tiny, white bikini. The bottom fit tightly against her skin and rode very high on top of her dark smooth hips, and the top cupped her breasts tightly.

"Oh God, so am I!" Zach said in response to her last statement.

"I take it you approve?"

"Oh yes, ohhh yes."

"Pervert!" she teased. "Do you know what the weather is for today?"

"It's supposed to be 83 degrees today."

"What about the water?"

"It might be a little nippy, but you sure aren't changing now!"

"Is that so?" she smirked.

She walked over and gave him a slight push, which caused him to fall back into a chair, willingly. She leaned down, letting her large breasts come directly into his view.

"There's just one little problem, Zach."

"Uh, what, what's that?" he stuttered, without moving his eyes from her chest.

"The bottom's okay, but if your friend doesn't have a good life vest, then I might lose this top. You wouldn't want that, would you?" Her voice was soft and sultry as she tugged lightly on the string at her cleavage.

"Uh, no. We wouldn't want to give everyone a free show," Zach answered, trying to regain some composure. "And yeah, he does have good life vests."

"Okay." She giggled and jumped to her feet, turned and walked straight out the door.

"Freakin' tease," Zach mumbled as his eyes followed her twisting buns. Then, as if icing the cake, her fingers looped under the bikini bottom at the top of her hips and slid all the way down pulling it out tight, then snapping it against her tanned body when she released it. She looked over her shoulder as Zach's head fell lifelessly back into the chair.

They put the soft top down on Zach's BMW and drove out to the Fox River as the sun beat down, warming the earth as previously promised. A beautiful eighteen–foot ski-nautique was waiting for them when they got to the marina. Zachery had learned how to water–ski in his early teens. While he didn't ski often, he'd always gone several times a month during the summer, keeping up some measure of expertise.

But it was Zach, not Taylor, who was surprised once they started skiing. She looked like a professional, using only one ski all afternoon. She slalomed back and forth with the grace of a swan, carving sheets of cool, clear water twenty feet into the air while Zach watched in amazement from the boat. Her skiing was fantastic, but that wasn't all of it.

She just seemed so perfect, so in sync with him. Zach felt alive when they were together, more so than in years. He was finally admitting it to himself openly. A moment didn't pass that warm thoughts of her didn't fill his heart. He felt good about everything. The clear, blue sky and the cool water soothed his nerves. He enjoyed the whole day without so much as one interruption. The outing helped him escape his disturbing worries for at least one day.

After tiring of the skiing, they spent the late afternoon hours relaxing and soaking up the remainder of the day's sun. Zach found a secluded area and beached the boat on a sand bank. They hardly spoke the rest of the afternoon. It was an unnecessary interruption. This was a tranquility they both needed desperately. Their hands lay clasped between them as both drifted in and out of a sun-induced slumber.

Later they drove back to Taylor's apartment to get cleaned up. Zachery, with some ideas of his own, followed her through the front door. Once inside, she tossed aside his shirt, which she'd been using as a cover-up. He watched her hips swinging back and forth as he followed her into the bedroom, reaching his arms around her petite waist and pulling her tight to him. Her bronzed stomach still radiated the sun's heat from earlier.

Taylor relished his touch, his strong hands felt so good around her. He pressed tightly against her, moving his hands to the bikini top, where his fingers pulled the tiny strings which were holding it tight against her chest. She allowed it to loosen and drop to the floor. Her fires had ignited far earlier in the day though, and she turned to face him, quickly removing the bottoms also. Zach started undressing, but it was too slow for her. Taylor wanted him now and tugged his clothes from him. Her hands quickly slid across his dark chest as she looked into his dazzling blue eyes. She wanted his body against hers.

Earlier in the day, Taylor had watched Zach climb into the boat after a long ski run. His muscles had been pumped from the exercise, and the water glistening on his chest and shoulders. At that moment, hours ago, the fantasies started. She had planned to make love to her man as soon as they returned. She took his hand and led him to her bed where she took complete control. They rolled in circles ripping the sheets into chaos as he bid to take the lead and become the aggressor. But Taylor would have none of it. She had him right where she wanted.

She lay on top of him, dipping her breasts down into his mouth, then leaning down kissing his neck and chest passionately. Both their hands clasped together tightly, and Taylor refused to let his go. Instead, she continued to allow his mouth to her breasts until she was ready to make love and guided him inside her. Their bodies tingled as she lifted herself off of him and then back down, slowly, then faster and faster. Finally the two lovers gasped for air as she brought them both to orgasm and collapsed onto his chest.

Without raising her head from his warm chest, he heard her say, "I love you, Zach Crawford." It was soft, but clear, and it was the first time either had dared to say it aloud.

He pulled her tight to his chest, now realizing that he could say it also. He had known too long without having the courage to tell her. Now it was time.

"I love you, Taylor."

Chapter
Twelve

The street running in front of Zach's apartment building was filled with cars. Sounds of car horns and pedestrians crossing were all around. A man stood at a far corner across from the entrance of the elegant building. Several passersby glanced his way in disgust, assuming he was another transient, homeless bum. His hair was long and blonde, but very stringy and dirty looking. The jeans he wore hung loosely on his thin frame. They appeared to be the same pair he'd been wearing for a week. And a ratty, worn–out, striped shirt was swinging freely in the wind with most of the buttons unfastened. It exposed his unimpressive skinny chest. His thin arms hung limp to his sides, several bruises at the joint. With the paleness and extreme, thin, drawn features, the only conclusion one could draw was that of drug use.

He paid no mind to the people scurrying by, but just stared intently at the huge glass entrance to the building across the street, Zach Crawford's building. His hand dug in a pocket and pulled out a watch and a crumpled newspaper article. He glanced at the paper momentarily. It was the article about Zachery's promotion at Global.

"Thought you were rid of me didn't ya, Crawford," he mumbled. "Well I found ya. . ."

He checked the time from the cheap watch which only had half a wrist band and slipped it easily back into the hip pocket of his ragged jeans. It was 9:40 A.M.. Zachery had been at work for more than an hour by this time.

The man smirked slightly and started across the busy street. He walked to the front of the building and looked in. A tall muscular black man wearing a uniform glared at him from the other side of the glass doors. The transient sighed with disinterest and walked on. The uniformed black man exited the building and watched him round the corner before returning to the lobby and taking his seat again. The blonde skinny man continued to walk down the block until he came to an alley behind the buildings.

He looked both ways and quickened his pace, entering the alleyway while pulling a keyring full of keys from the opposite pocket the watch had been in. A large green metal door came into view as he passed a maroon dumpster, overflowing with trash. The door was unmarked, but obviously belonged to Zach's building, with the styling up the backside matching that of the front of the building. The transient looking guy walked up to the door and inserted a key. It didn't work. He tried another with the same result. Obviously, he didn't know which key worked this lock, but six keys later he was successful. He chuckled aloud with delight.

The door squeaked slightly as he opened it and entered the building rather confidently. He boldly walked through the room, not at all like the criminal he must have been. It was a big storeroom with boxes thrown around. There were no windows and no lights, so he moved slowly while his eyes adjusted to the semi-darkness. At the far side of the room he entered a freight elevator and pressed 30, the floor Zach lived on. It rattled to life and slowly lifted him to that floor. Since only building maintenance personnel used this elevator, he had an uninterrupted ride. The door slid open at the top exposing a view of several large industrial washing machines. One of them was running, the others still. He peeked around the corner of the elevator door to find that the room was empty. His cocky attitude was again apparent as he stroked the long blonde hair out of one eye and checked the door leading to the plush hallway. It was also empty. The man walked quietly down the hall with just a hint of caution, but still not much. His grungy sneakers squeaked with every step until he stopped in front of one of the doors. It was Zachery Crawford's.

His ear pressed against the door searching for any signs of life inside. It seemed empty as he knew it should be. He pulled the keys from his pocket again. The same procedure was used for this lock. After five keys, he was in. He had broken into Zachery's lavish apartment and invaded his private world. That in itself was a delightful accomplishment for the bum.

As the transient entered the foyer, a confident strut overcame him. An obnoxious chuckle came from his mouth while his eyes surveyed the plush sunken living room. He walked around the entire perimeter and continued the survey. The condo was a showplace. Zach had spared no expense. Collector's paintings filled the walls; a contemporary sculpture sat in one corner; rich leather chairs and a large Chinese vase were in the other.

The intruder didn't seem like a common thief, though. He passed over these things, being either uneducated or uninterested in them, maybe both. He jumped over the back and into the middle of the pit style couch situated in the sunken middle of the room.

"This is alright, Zach," he said, indicating his approval to an empty room. Then he laughed again, even wilder.

Suddenly, as quickly as it started, the laughter subsided completely. A focused look replaced the grin on his face. He jumped off the couch and scanned the room. His eyes caught momentarily on the drawers of the coffee and end tables. He darted to them and inspected the contents of each drawer. There was nothing of much interest in them. A book and notepad were the only contents of one. Another had only a few old receipts from six–month old purchases and a notepad, pencils and so on.

The intruder made his way to a doorway on the left side of the room. It was a bedroom that looked untouched since moving furniture in. Another door on the left side was pulled closed. He pushed it open fearlessly and found that it was Zachery's office.

His expression seemed to perk up. Now he was getting somewhere. He entered the room and went straight behind the desk to pilfer through the drawers. The middle one had only notepads, pens and pencils. He opened the large bottom drawer on the left. It had a small firebox to protect important papers. The latch was closed, but Zach never bothered to remove the key. He closed it to protect from fire not theft, and the key turned easily, unlocking the box. The man pulled a handful of papers out and strewed them across the desk. He scrutinized each one for a long time. Most of the papers were stock certificates and bonds. Zach owned many large blocks of stock, including several thousand shares of Global which had been given to him as bonuses. His sizable portfolio also included around twenty thousand dollars in government bonds. The man moved on to a passbook that showed another twenty thousand in regular savings. He was not knowledgeable in stocks, but this information thrilled him. He mentally figured the value of Zach's investments and guessed them to be one hundred fifty to two hundred thousand, even though he had no clue as to value of the stocks.

After viewing several more less interesting documents, the blonde-headed man neatly arranged the papers and put them back in the firebox. He didn't steal a thing! He was sure to close the desk drawer and put the chair back as he found it, then pulled the door closed again as he went to search the rest of the house.

A disgusted frown covered his face as he roamed the living room again, looking at the spectacular lake view through the glass wall. Envy and jealousy filled his veins. Crawford didn't deserve this life. But just maybe, his life could be stolen away.

He ambled to the other side of the apartment where he found the master bedroom with its raised king size bed. The satin sheets were wrinkled up and loosely thrown over the mattress.

"So this is where you're bangin' her," the man mumbled to himself. "I sure wouldn't mind gettin' to know that little piece of ass myself."

The rest of the room was relatively clean. The trespasser checked the dresser and chest of drawers for anything else of value, but found only clothing. Then he spotted the nightstands on either side of the bed. He skipped up the step, even with the bed, and reached for the drawer. It was the same drawer that housed the gun that had upset Taylor. The .38 caliber wasn't a big handgun, but enough to scare her. It had been in the same spot since the first night Zachery spent in this apartment, not even touched since then.

Suddenly, as his cold hand grasped the handle, a loud click rang from the living room. He spun around to see that the front door was wide open with the corner of a cart was being pushed through the doorway at that very instant. His heart jumped. Now this was excitement. Fear never even crossed his demented mind. He could plow over the person and run. This wasn't really a problem, but he didn't want to be caught. Zach couldn't find out about this. Instinctively he dropped to the floor, and with no other options, rolled under the bed. With the bed raised a step, the skirt was the only thing hiding his presence.

He slithered forward and leaned his head sideways to peek out between the satin bed skirt and the floor. Much to his pleasure, a young Latino girl in a uniform was standing in the living room. Her back was to him as she softly pushed the front door closed. Long jet black hair hung completely straight to about the middle of her back. She was relatively tall and very thin, built like a model.

'Nice butt,' he thought.

As she turned to the cart, he admired the front view. She was a typical Latin girl with a beautiful dark complexion and big brown eyes. Her uniform was that of a cleaning service, mostly white with some black accents. The dress rode up her thighs as she reached down for a dust rag on the cart, and under the bed the bum strained to see up it. Much to his disappointment, however, she held herself very ladylike, keeping her knees together as they bent.

He lay absolutely still while she went about her work throughout the apartment. Soon he glanced at his watch and saw that he had been stuck under the bed for over twenty minutes. Occasionally she would pass by the doorway, but other than that he couldn't tell what was happening. After another ten minutes, she moved to the kitchen, which was visible from his vantage point. He watched her hair swing from side to side as she cleaned. His interest was finally waning when something else happened. While leaning over the table, she bumped a half eaten bowl of cereal with her hand. It catapulted through the air and hit her square in the chest, spraying soggy wheat flakes and milk around the room and soaking the entire front of her dress. She screamed with surprise as the bowl thumped her chest and milk ran down the inside and out of the previously white dress. It was now somewhat tan colored from the cereal-browned milk. Her surprise turned to anger and she began to curse under her breath in Spanish.

Under the bed still, the man fought a burst of laughter off, while the young girl cleaned the mess up and mopped the floor. She tugged at the sopping front of the dress. It was obviously beginning to get sticky feeling against her soft skin. His interest rekindled.

After the mess was taken care of, she sighed disgustedly while examining the developing stain on her uniform. Suddenly she walked straight toward him. Surprised, his head jerked back from the crack of the opening in the bedskirt he had been using. She entered the bedroom and turned to her right into the bathroom. His interest was undivided now as he hoped his guess was right. And it was.

The door was left open. After all, she believed she was alone. She stood in front of the sink facing the mirror and began unbuttoning the dress. Once it was undone to her waist, she slid the top over her shoulders and the uniform fell to the floor.

It was suddenly very warm under the bed. The man's heart quickened as he watched.

Her arms reached behind her and unhooked the small lacy bra she was wearing. She pulled it off and tossed it into the sink. Then she grabbed the dress, added it and started filling the sink with water.

From underneath the bed, the man watched her intently as she scrubbed the stains. She was magnificent. Her hair lay against the dark bare skin of her back. The only remaining article of clothing she wore was a pair of very high cut white panties from which her round ass hung out of very appealingly.

'*She's hot!*' He was busy convincing himself. '*She needs a man.*'

He wanted to throw her to the ground and have his way with her. She needed a man. He could show her what she needed.

He had convinced himself to jump out and fuck her hard. But that would screw up everything. What about the money? He had to control himself. There was a plan, and she would only complicate it. He could restrain himself. '*But that bitch doesn't know what she's missing!*'

With the clothes washed out, she hung them up to dry, then walked out into the bedroom. A chill came over him as she walked to the bed. He felt as though his mouth was watering like a hungry animal. Her young pointed breasts were as dark as the rest of her body. She was just thin enough that her ribcage was faintly visible. The white panties scooped down in the front to just barely cover her bushy crotch. She turned and sat on the bed. His restraint was fading. She stroked her hand up and down the satin sheets, while he watched through a cheval mirror that he spotted in the corner of the room. Her eyes were closed as she wrapped the sheets and her arms tightly around her smooth body.

His expression changed. Maybe she was hot for Crawford. Maybe she wanted to screw him! What the hell did she see in him? The man became irrational. '*Damn whore! He's no man. If she wants a real man, I can show her what a real man can do for her!*' His eyes squinted nearly shut, the stringy blonde hair hanging over half his face. His breathing became strained with rage, his body beginning to shake with fury. '*That's it. I'll show the foreign cunt.*'

He was just about to start out from beneath the bed when she jumped up and started cleaning again. She was completely naked except for the tiny lacy panties, and her firm breasts jiggled while she bounced around the room. As she made the bed, she bent down to tuck a corner in only inches from his silent watchful eye. He peered out. Her stance was not as feminine as before. She was on the balls of her feet with legs spread wide. He stared at her crotch only a foot away, but the desire was gone. She was a tramp. She would fuck anything. After all, she was probably fucking him. *'Bitch! What kind of a tramp is she? I should show her what I got. She'd stop her whoring ways then. I'd keep her satisfied. But, she don't deserve it. I got better things to do than pleasure this Mexican bitch!'*

The young cleaning girl thought nothing of her stance. After all, she was alone. She could finish cleaning, and by then the uniform would be almost dry. And it was true. She had seen Zachery around the building. He was handsome, successful, thoughtful. She often wondered what it would be like to be his lady. It must be wonderful to live like him. She would be treated like a queen. But, of course, she had never slept with him. They had rarely even spoken when passing in the halls. It was just a young girl's fantasy, nothing more.

Her bare body hopped about the room as she finished cleaning. The man, still under the bed, spitefully watched her unclothed flesh. He still longed to prove to her that he was better than Zach, but remained silent. He just kept repeating to himself over and over, *'two hundred thousand dollars. . .two hundred thousand dollars. . .two hundred thousand dollars. . .'*

He had been cornered in the same spot for an hour and a half when she was finally finished straightening the place. She strutted back to the bathroom confidently. As the intruder watched her dress, he felt the desire rising within him. Yet she couldn't be forgiven for wanting HIM, wanting Zach. He wouldn't give her the satisfaction. After all, Mr. high and mighty Zachery Crawford had a lesson to learn. He might not be so desirable without all his money. . .Just another fuckin' pathetic loser.

And this man had a plan. Crawford would pay.

The Latin girl finished buttoning her uniform and straightened around the sink. He watched her butt twist as she left the room and went to the cart. She grabbed the front door and pulled the cart through it, leaving him alone, finally. He rolled out from beneath the mattress and stood beside the bed. It was the same spot he had occupied when she interrupted. He stretched momentarily and scanned the neat room.

He had forgotten the nightstands and their drawers. Only three feet away lay the .38 caliber, still silently stashed in the back of the drawer.

It was time to go. Zachery's portfolio of investments was plenty of ammo. He wouldn't need anything else. His plan was ready to lunge into action.

He took a long look at the neatly made bed. His sick mind pictured the Latino maid lying naked, her legs spread wide. Taylor also appeared on the soft satin sheets. She begged him to come to her and fulfill her fantasies.

All in due time. . .All in due time. They would have to wait until he was done with Crawford.

He checked the hall and left the way he had come.

Chapter
Thirteen

There was a soft noise in the background. Zachery didn't hear it at first, but it continued getting louder and louder. He reached for the alarm instinctively, but soon discovered this was not the source of the clamor. At last he realized that he'd been asleep, and the noise was the telephone waking him.

Taylor lay next to him with her head resting on his arm, which was wrapped around her. She was still asleep, so he pulled his arm out from under her and carefully got up, trying not to wake her. It had been very late when they finally got back to Zach's last night. With the movement of the bed, she frowned and squirmed a little before settling again. Zach didn't bother with trying to find something to cover himself as he ran into the living room to answer the phone, which must have rung twenty times by now. He picked up the receiver with one hand while he rubbed the sleep from his eyes with the other.

"Hello," he said in a gruff, sleepy voice.

The phone was silent for a moment. Only some background noise came through the receiver.

"Hello," Zach mumbled again in his deep morning voice.

"Zachery Crawford, please," came a voice over the line, very slow and deliberate.

Zach's eyes opened wide, instantly. The caller was on a pay phone somewhere judging from the car horns and voices in the background. He was able to discern the caller's voice, though. It had no peculiar quality to distinguish it from any other, but it sounded very familiar to him just the same. It frightened him. It sounded like a voice from a part of his past that he didn't want to remember. It was a voice from the dream that had haunted him over the years, only now it was back in his real life, not just his dreams.

Zachery was silenced, unable to answer. He told himself that he was just being paranoid as he summoned up the courage to acknowledge who he was.

"Yes, this is he."

"Well," the voice laughed. "How ya doin', Zach, old buddy?"

Zachery couldn't ignore it this time. It WAS a voice from the past, the voice of the leader in the dream. He was so shocked that he couldn't answer.

"What's wrong?" the voice said with the same slang it had long ago. "Don't you like hearing from an old school buddy?" He paused again, chuckling. "You know who I am, don't cha pal?"

Zachery knew that he had to say something. It wasn't the leader himself that frightened Zach. It was the ugly memory he was associated with, the same ugly memory from his dreams.

"Yeah, Curry," he said sternly, calling him by his last name only. "What do you want?"

Zachery already knew that whatever he wanted, it was trouble. "Uh, just hadn't talked to ya in awhile. I wanted to see how you were doin'." All the while, Curry continued to chuckle each time he spoke.

Zachery remained silent.

"I saw your promotion in the paper a few weeks ago and decided to look ya up to congratulate you."

"Thanks a lot, Curry. Now if that's all, I'm busy." He tried to hang the phone up before Curry caught him again.

"No, no, wait a second Zach, old boy," he said with that now annoying chuckle. "That's no way to treat an old friend, is it?"

Zach did not reply.

"Okay, okay, Zach. You got me." Curry had spoken as though Zach dragged the hidden reason from him. "There was another reason I called. I need to ask you just a little favor, old pal."

"What is it?" Zach said to him firmly, while truly he was very worried.

"I've got some financial difficulties right now. I been out of work for awhile, you know how hard it is to find a job these days, pal." He paused momentarily. "Well. Maybe ya don't. Anyway, I haven't worked for a spell, and I thought that since you were such a big man now at that fancy computer place that you could make a small contribution to help tide me over for awhile."

"Oh, come on, Curry. You've got to be kidding. You think I'm gonna give you money?"

Curry interrupted him sharply, "C'mon Zach, I'm serious. You're a successful businessman now. I just thought that you wouldn't mind helping an old friend. . .One that you share so many memories with."

He thought about it for a second before answering. *'How could Curry come back after all these years? This is nothing short of blackmail. That's what that goddamn memories slur is about.'*

"Okay, all right," he said disgustedly. "If it'll get you off my back. How much do you need?"

"Oh thanks, pal," Curry said sarcastically. "I knew you'd come through. I swear I won't come around any more asking for anything."

"How much?" Zach repeated louder.

Curry's voice answered. This time there was no snickering or chuckling in the background. It had been re-placed with a harsh, serious tone as he spoke slowly and clearly.

"Two. . .hundred. . .thousand. . .dollars."

"What? Are you crazy?" Zach screamed.

Curry answered back calmly, "No, not crazy, but serious, dead serious."

"Well, I can't help you, Curry. I don't have that kind of money, and even if I did, I wouldn't give it to you."

"Oh, but that's not true, Zach. I been watching you now for several weeks. I've seen the building you work in, I've seen your fancy car, the furniture in that apartment of yours doesn't look too cheap either."

"What do you mean? When have you seen it? How did you get my number?" The questions poured out.

"Well, that was easy. Your secretary barely hesitated to give it to me. And that poor fellow that's in the hospital now. . .. He was so kind as to let me borrow a key to your apartment."

Zach was getting very nervous. He knew Curry was talking about Paul, the garage watchman, who always carried a master key in case of emergencies. Curry had been snooping through his apartment. He was screwing with his life. It had seemed in the past that Curry was strange, but Zach never imagined him such a crazed and desperate criminal.

"Curry, I'm serious. I don't have that kind of money."

"Zachery, Zachery, I'm sure the police would be very interested in our little secret."

"You wouldn't," Zachery said trying to bluff him. "They wouldn't believe you if you did."

"I'm sure an anonymous phone call with a few facts thrown in would do something. Besides, even if they couldn't pin it on you, don't you think that it could ruin your career? Plus, you'd lose all your high and mighty friends, including that cute little fuck you been hanging out with."

"What do you mean? Who?" Zach bluffed again.

"Oh, don't play that. The hot blonde."

"Leave her out of this, Curry." Zach was enraged.

Curry just laughed at him.

Zachery decided to play his hand. "Curry, what makes you think that you wouldn't go to jail with me? You're not exactly innocent, keeping quiet all these years."

"C'mon buddy, I could come up with an alibi and have some of my lowly friends testify for me. Even if I did get caught, I bet I'd walk if I agreed to testify against you, such a pillar of our fine community."

Curry stopped and listened for Zachery's reaction. But Zachery had broken out into a cold sweat. He couldn't believe this was happening to him, and he knew that he couldn't do a thing about it. Curry was just crazy enough to go to the police with his story. Zach had worked hard to get where he was. He couldn't afford to start over. This whole thing was crazy, unimaginable. What if Curry did something to Taylor? He couldn't stand the thought of that.

"Well, Zachery. What'll it be?" Curry demanded.

"Curry, where am I supposed to get that much money? That's a hell of a lot of money." His voice was shaky.

"I'll bet you have a lot of rich friends. Yeah, pretty good credit. Stocks and bonds. You'll think of a way." Curry continued to torment him.

"You've gotta give me awhile. It'll take time to find that kind of money." Zachery was almost frantic.

"I can understand that, you've got a week. If you don't have it by then, you're asking for trouble. And don't think that I won't give it to you."

"I'll have it."

"All right, buddy," Curry said, with the chuckling voice again. "I've gotta go now. Oh, and by the way give her a good morning fuck for me, too." He laughed loudly and hung the phone up in Zach's ear.

Zachery put his head down on the table, bewildered. What could he do? He didn't have THAT much money. This thing could ruin his entire life. It was a terrible mistake he made so many years ago. Maybe if he had come clean then, his life may have been spared the dreadful consequences.

"What was that about?"

He jerked his head up and turned toward the bedroom. There stood Taylor. She had thrown one of his dress shirts around her. It was left unbuttoned and fell open several inches in the front, pulled to the sides by her large breasts. He slowly eyed her body as he walked across the room to her, pulling the shirt open and drawing her towards him until their naked bodies met inside of it. He rubbed his hands across the smooth dark skin of her back and let the warmth radiate from her body into his. It seemed to relax him.

"Is something wrong?   What was that phone call about so early in the morning?" she repeated.

"Why? Did it wake you? Could you hear me?" His voice was still shaky.

"Oh, I was about half awake. I didn't hear anything, but I could hear you raising your voice. Sorry, I didn't mean to eavesdrop."

"Oh no, honey. I just didn't want to wake you up. It was just a prank call, and I got a little bit upset."

"You're sure there's nothing wrong?" she asked again.

He looked into her clear, blue eyes wishing that he could tell her. But he had to do what Curry said. If he didn't, and something happened to Taylor, he wouldn't be able to stand it. She was the only thing that was still right in his life. As far as he knew, half the people he worked with were crooks, the project was starting to fall off its schedule, and he was about to go broke; However, he might be able to liquify some investments and borrow the rest to come up with enough.

'Who does that son of a bitch think he is making me pay for a mistake that I made years ago, as if the dream of it isn't torment enough, especially when he had as much to do with it as me. Why should he get off the hook? Why is everything falling apart now?' he asked himself. *'Things were great only weeks ago: first a promotion, then a raise, then the best thing to happen to me in years. I'll do whatever it takes to keep you safe, Taylor,'* he said to himself. Then he answered her.

"No, I'm fine. Let's go back to bed."

As they lay down, Zach pulled the nightstand drawer open.

"What are you doing?" Taylor asked, as she pulled the sheets over her.

"Just getting an aspirin," Zach answered, while his eyes peered nervously at the gun pushed to the back of the drawer. "Let's go back to sleep."

He slid the drawer closed and wrapped his arm around Taylor, pulling her to his side, then leaned to her and gently kissed her forehead. She smiled slightly, her eyes remaining closed.

Chapter Fourteen

The pressures were finally taking their toll on Zachery. His head hung low as he plodded off to work, and his eyes were sunk deep into their sockets with deep, dark rings underneath, due to lack of sleep caused by the worsening dream, if he was able to fall asleep in the first place. And every waking moment his mind raced with concerns about Curry and the money he was demanding. The computer break-ins almost seemed trivial now in the light of Zachery's new problems, unless, that is, Curry was involved. But then again, he didn't have the brains for something like that. Zach didn't like unfinished business, though. So the concern was still there. Yes, his intent was still to resolve this problem for his employers...and for himself. Zachery Crawford was not going to allow his personal problems to interfere with the career he had struggled to build. Besides, if

that problem was gone, one less item would be weighting
him down.

He walked through the lobby at work, ignoring the friends
and colleagues who had spoken to him every day for years.
The guidance that his team of programmers looked to him
for was not there. They frowned to each other as he blindly
walked past them, making a straight line yet again for the
solitude of his closed office.

Taylor noticed it more than anyone. But she hadn't
known Zachery Crawford for long. There was no way for
her to know if this was his true self or not. Was she wrong
about him? Maybe he wasn't the secure, successful man
who had filled her body with tingling infatuation and love for
a month. Or was it her? She tried not to think of this possibility, but yet it was there, pulling at her contented heart as
though trying to spoil her happiness. It could be that Zach
didn't love her after all. Maybe their relationship was
bogging him down to where he was in a constant state of
depression. He could be trying to alienate her, run her off
so that it was somehow her fault when she finally broke it off
with him.

Still, he was different at home. He continued to treat
her well. They lay in each other's arms for hours on end.
The sex had tapered off, though. Instead they talked and
laughed, and they shared the same bed. That was all as
wonderful as it had been from the start. But he wasn't
sleeping well due to the dreams, the dreams that Zachery
still kept a secret. She would never be able to help him
without knowing the source of his anguish, so she held and
comforted him when he would awaken at night.

Cowboy Bob was standing in the computer room. His
eyes followed Zach as he was walking through to the other
door leading to his office. His steps echoed quickly over the
hard tile flooring. Bob saw the drawn worrisome look
plastered across Zachery's face. He had never seen his
boss, his friend so unhappy and so withdrawn. Zach had

always treated him with respect and kindness. His friend was hurting, and watching it hurt him.

Bob's eyes stopped following Zach part way across the room as something distracted him. His pupils resized, as he refocused on the background. Taylor stood on the far side of the computer room watching Zach walk through, just as Bob was. His expression shifted to one of annoyance, no, even outrage. It must be her. It had taken only a month for her to do this to him. The little bitch really scrambled his brain with those short skirts and big tits. Bob hated to admit it, but he too found Taylor extremely attractive. This, however, did not excuse her disruption of the serenity that had been enjoyed by Zachery's group. *She might be a looker, but something ain't right if she's doin' this to him.* They didn't need this cute little wrench thrown into their gears.

He sighed deeply with disgust and made his way across the room to confront her.

"What the HELL is going on here!" he demanded of her.

"What do you mean?" she asked. For a moment she genuinely thought she had made some drastic error or something of that nature related to her work.

"Him!" Bob pointed to Zach's back, just as it disappeared behind the door on the other side of the computer room.

Taylor looked back at Zach again herself. Only now did she realize that Bob blamed her for Zachery's disposition. She jerked her head back.

"What are you asking ME for?" she glared back at him.

"I've known Zach for several years," Bob lectured. "He's been a good friend from the beginning. I can't stand what's happening to him. I've never seen him like this before."

"It's not my fault, Bob," Taylor interrupted.

"He didn't start acting like this until y'all started goin' out."

"So what!"

"So what is wrong with him?"

"I don't know! But our private life is none of your business."

"You came in here a month ago. . .started messin' with his head. . .and now guess what. You're sittin' purtty."

"You bastard!" she answered, with a stifled yell. "Who do you think you are? I love that man. I wish I knew what WAS wrong with him."

"Did you ever stop to think maybe it was you?"

"He swears that nothing's wrong. I've asked him every day for a week. If he asked me to, I'd leave today. I'd leave him. I'd leave this job. But he hasn't. He says he needs me. He says he loves me."

Taylor lowered her head to her chest. Tears began to swell in the corners of her eyes. But she refused to raise her head and give Bob the satisfaction of beating up on her. He watched as she raised her hand to wipe the tears before they could run down her soft cheeks. She seemed vulnerable. . .Not the ruthless she-devil he had concocted in his mind. He didn't even know her yet. How could he accuse her of this behavior? He might have been too hard on her. Maybe he was wrong about her. . .Anyway, she was right, their relationship wasn't his business. In his best voice, Bob tried to muster up an apology. He was unaccustomed to this, but stumbled through it anyway, now that his guilt began to grow.

"Look. . .look Taylor, I'm sorry." She did nothing. "I guess I was wrong."

"You're damn right you're wrong," she spurted back at him, finally raising her head.

"I'm really sorry. I didn't mean to take it out on you. It's just that seeing Zach this way really gets to me."

"Yeah, me too. He's changed so much in just the last two weeks."

"You don't have any idea what's buggin' him?" Bob was polite and caring now as he rephrased his question.

"No, he just says he's got a lot on his mind and not to worry. . ." She trailed off.

"I can't hardly believe it's the Lakeshore project. Zach loves his work, he thrives on the pressure."

"Well he must have pressure from someone or something else then, Bob."

"Taylor," he started after a long pause. "I don't know what to do. If you find out what's wrong, I'll help if I can. And really. . .I'm sorry I jumped you. I was dead wrong."

"I'm glad Zach has a friend who cares so much for him," she answered, trying to accept his apology.

"Thanks for understanding." He spoke softly, then lowered his head walking away, a bit of shame trickling through his body.

Determination coursed through her veins. It was time to find out what was eating at Zach. . .and. . .what was testing the strength of their love. Taylor strode across the room, through the door and down the plush and quiet hallway. When she reached the door to his office, she inhaled deeply and threw it open.

"Next Wednesday!" Zach yelled. "I can't wait that long!"

His back was turned to her and the phone pinned to his right ear. Taylor stood silently in the doorway. He obviously didn't hear her come in.

"I need that money by tomorrow," he continued. "Isn't there any way you can speed it up?"

He paused, listening to the unknown voice on the other side of the line.

"I've kept all my accounts and investments with your bank for years now. Can't you make any exceptions?"

He paused for another second, listening. He began pacing, but when he turned back and spotted Taylor, his expression went blank.

"Uh. . .I'll have to call back. Bye." He ended the phone call immediately.

"What's going on, Zach?" Taylor asked with a frightened voice.

"How long have you been standing there?" he demanded.

"Zach?"

Her concern caused her voice to shudder. Zach realized how scared she was. He didn't mean to do that to the woman he loved.

"I'm sorry, Taylor, what do you need?" He tried to change the subject.

"WHAT DO I NEED?" she mocked. "I need to know what the hell is wrong with you."

"Nothing. . .I don't know what you mean."

"Are you in trouble, Zach? Please tell me, I love you, and this is driving me crazy."

"I'm not in any trouble, honey."

"Who was on the phone then?"

"It was just my bank."

"You sounded pretty upset!"

Zach knew he had to give her some explanation, so he decided to lie. It wasn't the right thing to do, but the truth was too ugly to reveal.

"Okay, it's no big deal."

"Yes?" she probed on.

"A guy I know called last weekend. We go back a long way."

"Go on. . ."

"He's had a hard time of things lately. He called to see if I would help him out a little."

Of course, this was stretching things a bit. The help Curry wanted was to the tune of two hundred thousand dollars.

"So what's wrong with that? What's he want?"

"He wants me to loan him some money. I said I would."

"Is that a good idea, Zach?" Taylor tried to be helpful and constructive with her line of questioning.

"Yeah. . .He's good for it. He seems like he really needs it," Zach answered as his inner self snarled at the thought of this deception.

"Well, he's your friend. I think it's nice of you to help him out. Do you mind if I ask how much he wants?"

Zach turned nonchalantly away, so Taylor couldn't see his face as he answered.

"Uh. . .Several. . .uh. . .thousand dollars," he answered walking toward his office window, his back still to her.

"Don't you have it?" Taylor asked surprised that a man such as Zach might not have a lot of money at his fingertips.

"I guess so. . .At least in CD's and funds. . .that sort of thing."

Taylor sensed his discomfort with this subject. Maybe it was too early to press him about money matters. He didn't want to tell her any details. It was obvious. His several thousand dollars might be ten or twenty thousand dollars. I guess that might be a bit harder to lay your hands on at the blink of an eye. It was his money, though, to do with what he pleased.

"Do you want any help?" she asked, while trying not to bruise his ego with such an offer.

"No, no," he quickly responded. "I'll get it. I just have to get through some red tape at the bank. . .You know how it is."

"Yeah, I guess."

Disgusted with himself, Zach eased Taylor's worries and quickly ushered her out his door.

Chapter
Fifteen

Zach turned from the door, sighing from relief. He had lied to her, and she had believed and trusted him. He hoped it wasn't the wrong thing to do.

A loud beep rang through the silent office. It was the intercom of his phone.

"Zach. . .line 12 please," a soft voice came over.

"Okay, thanks," Zach answered on the way around his large desk. *'Hopefully that's the bank calling back with good news, if you could call it that.'*

"Zach Crawford," he said strongly into the receiver.

"Hello Zachery," a slow deliberate voice echoed.

"Curry."

"That's right, buddy boy, it's me."

Zach's heart dropped right into the pit of his empty stomach. *'Not again. . .How many times is he going to call and torment me. I'm doing all I can. . .I still have a couple days. He's insane. He just wants to make me squirm. Will I ever be free of him, even after he gets the money? He's a bloodsucker, like a tick on a dog. Always was, always will be.'*

The fact remained though, Zach had to deal with him or pay the piper for his past sins.

"What do you want NOW?" Zach roared, but with restraint enough so as not to be heard outside the room.

"Do you have my money?" Curry was cold and direct.

"I didn't have it yesterday. I didn't have it the day before. And I don't have it today!"

"Don't you go smartin' off to me, man, I'm givin' you plenty of time."

"You said I had a week."

"I'm just keepin' tabs on ya, Crawford," Curry interrupted. "You better be gettin' it before the end of the week."

"I'm trying. . .I'm trying. But I don't know if I can get it that quick. My bank isn't helping me much."

That news sent Curry into a rage as if unleashing a hungry lion.

"Now you listen to me, Crawford," he screamed uncontrollably. "I've kept quiet for all these years. It was your fuck up that night. I could've ratted you out for it. . .but I didn't. . .Instead, I protected you like a brother. How did you repay me?"

He waited for an answer, but Zach did not speak.

"I said, 'How did you repay me for my loyalty, Crawford?' You took off. You thought if you left town, you could just run away. Everything would be right back to normal. Fuck me, huh. . .Fuck the rest of us. . .Fuck that night in the woods. You'll just go to the city and have a great fucking life while the rest of us live with your mistake. Well it doesn't work like that. You're not getting off scot–free on it. You owe me! You could've stayed in touch, but you thought you could shit on us; go to your fancy job, drive your fancy cars and fuck your fancy bitches. And all the while I'm rotting in the gutter with YOUR guilt. You should be here, not me! You owe ME!"

"It's not my fault if you never did anything with your life." Zach responded to the accusations. "You think I owe you just because I'm successful?"

"You wouldn't be so damn successful if I hadn't helped you in the woods that night. You'd be rotting in jail somewhere gettin' buttfucked by some big fat rapist. But you're not, you're screwing that Williams bitch. Maybe I should buttfuck her since that kind of crap probably turns your stomach!"

"Leave her out of this, you son of a bitch!"

"Oooh. A sensitive subject, huh?"

"She has nothing to do with any of this. Just leave her alone, Curry."

"I'll leave her alone." He paused for what seemed an eternity. "As long as you get that money."

"I will. I will."

"If you don't, she'll be the first one I tell the story to." He paused again. "But ya know, I've noticed how protective you are about her. Maybe I'll tell your boss first. . .Yeah. . . Maybe I won't tell the bitch at all. I'll just show her what a real man could do for her. She wouldn't be happy with your mushy ways after I got done with her."

"IF YOU TOUCH HER, I'LL KILL YOU!!"

"Ha," Curry laughed spitefully. "I won't have to if you do what you're supposed to."

"I'll have it. I swear." Zach's voice carried a noticeably desperate tone.

"What about your bank?"

"I can get it. Don't worry about the bank. I'll get the money."

"YOU—DAMN—WELL—BETTER," Curry exploded one last time.

Zach sat speechless, everything quiet except for heavy breathing slipping through the phone as Curry caught his breath. Finally the receiver clicked down, and the line was silent.

He was deranged, really deranged. Zach had never imagined him this unbalanced. He was always strange, but. . .

His account of the past was far different than that of Zach's. He HAD been there that fateful night. But he wasn't the pillar of support. He was involved, too. He was the leader of the fraternity. The whole plan was originally his idea. But then things went wrong, and what happened next was the source of the haunting memories that invaded Zach's sleep.

What had Curry done with his life? It wasn't guilt that kept him down. He was a loser, and Zach always knew it. Zach imagined him on the other side of their conversation. He was standing in a dirty public phone booth, one of the windows broken out. He had the same blonde hair, but it was longer, greasier. It hung down to his shoulders. He was wearing a baggy stained tank top with his shoulders and arms hanging out unimpressively. Cheap jeans hung loosely off his hips. He was extremely skinny and pale. His eyes were drawn back in his head. He used drugs and drank heavily. His worn body betrayed him. Jobs had come and gone, but he never held one more than a month or so.

Curry slammed the phone down and slid the phone booth door open. He blundered uncaringly across the street, kicking a beer can in the gutter as we went. Then he glanced up as he stepped onto the sidewalk. An old twelve-story brick building partially blocked the sunlight. It was Curry's home for now. He was kicked out of many as would be from this one soon. A heavy wooden door with chipped dull black paint lay wide open, leading into the building. He bounced through it and started up a narrow flight of stairs. They were dimly lit by a single hanging bulb on the landing of each floor. His careless walk was magnified as his shoes shuffled loudly on the gritty unpainted steps.

Curry turned a corner and headed to his fifth floor room. The hallway was short, a dirty broken window supplying the only light from the far end. A baby's cry came from behind the first door, and a young man yelled at his woman behind another one.

Finally Curry entered his room. It was uncarpeted also. The room was small. A twin bed was pushed into the left corner, its boxsprings uncovered by a skirt. One window looked over the little driven street below. No curtains hung from it, only a pull down blind. Curry plopped down on the bed and turned on a small 13" television across the room. The picture was slightly snowy, but he was content for now.

Content. Zach tensed up with his images of this loser. It must be how he lived. There was no doubt. Curry was a simpleton whose luck was soon to change. He would soon be content to live quite well at Zach's expense. He wouldn't feel guilt. He wouldn't give it a second thought. That was Curry. His entire life was lived at the expense of others. He was a selfish, useless shell of a man.

Zach sat in the high-backed leather chair behind his huge desk in his huge office. The reality was that he would pay it. There was no choice, never was. Since the first call last weekend, Zach had no other options but to submit to Curry's demands. He knew it then, he knew it now. With every harassing call it was more clear. There was absolutely no question. Each call was more hostile than the last. The man was crazy. Zach was scared of him. Curry was a desperate man with an easy money plan. He would carry through with every threat made. Taylor included. . .

Chapter
Sixteen

There were eight or ten guys sitting around the fire on a fallen log, on a rock and on the ground. They were young men, probably about 20 years old. They all wore faded jeans, a varied style of T-shirts from various popular designers. It was quiet all around them, except for some hard rock music blaring undiscernibly from a pickup truck parked about 25 yards away. They were deep in the woods, somewhere away from all civilization, and all of them were very loud, yelling and laughing at each other. One threw an empty bottle into the fire, crashing it against a rock. It was obvious that they had all been drinking for some time and were quite drunk.

Zachery looked across the area slowly before focusing back on the large fire a few yards in front of him. His vision blurred momentarily. The heat was drying his eyes, causing him to blink often. He raised a fresh beer to his mouth and guzzled a large portion. Then one of them said something.

"Are you ready, pussy?"

The boy seemed to be the leader of the group. Blonde hair hung to one side almost completely over his right eye. He seemed to be an all American type, yet unconventional, a sort of rebel. His statement was directed to a guy on the other side of the fire, sitting alone. His age was around 18, a few years younger than the others. The loner was the only one of the bunch not drunk. The boy shook his head, trying to hide his fear.

"Okay, guys," said the leader. "The wimp says he's ready to go. Zach, you and Jimmy grab him."

The entire group broke into a hysterical laughter.

"All right, Curry," Zach slurred back.

They all jumped up, grabbing their drinks and stumbling away from the fire. Zach and Jimmy each grabbed an arm of the boy and began to pull him with them. The leader walked over to them and slowly put on a dark satin jacket with an emblem and three letters across the back. He took a white bandanna from his forehead and used it to blindfold the young man.

"So you want to be one of us. . .Well, you have to make it through tonight first, boy." The leader yelled to the rest. "Let's go!"

A loud cheer rose from the group as they began walking down a small path away from the light of the still burning fire. A few of them used flashlights to show the way even though their erratic drunken walk caused the beams of light to swing wildly off the path. Zach and Jimmy brought up the rear pulling the other boy. The boy gave no resistance, however. He wanted to be there. His fear was fairly well hidden, but everyone knew he was worried. There was no turning back now, though. He had put up with their petty crap all week. Now they had one last test (or trick), and they would be done. He would be a member of their fraternity.

Zach leaned over to the boy and said, "You're in for a night to remember!"

The young Zachery and his friends pulled and yanked on the young boy purposely, laughing and tormenting him. By now the whole group was so drunk that they stumbled over each other and weaved on and off of the path as they tried to walk. One slipped to the ground in a muddy patch, but no bother.

After a short time, the path ended, turning into a patch of short, thick undergrowth. This undergrowth surrounded a small dirt clearing with two or three small trees scattered about it. The new moon poured its bright light over them as they pulled the young boy to a larger tree in the center of the field and unbound him for a moment. One of his wrists had begun bleeding from the yanking and pulling during the trip through the woods.

The boy opposite Zach laughed and whispered, "You'd better hope nothin' gets a whiff of that. You know there's all kinds of wild animals scattered through these woods."

Zach wrapped the boy's arms around the tree, retying the ropes to his bleeding wrists. He winced slightly as the rough grain of the rope grated at his injured wrists. Meanwhile, the group gathered around the boy with the leader stepping toward him to speak. He pushed the long blonde hair out of his eyes and smiled at the boy.

"Okay, boy, you know what you have to do. You have to get loose from there and be back at the campus by dawn. If you make it, you're one of us. If you don't. . .," he paused and laughed wildly for what seemed like an endless amount of time. "If you don't, you better hope that someone finds you before you starve to death wrapped around this tree."

The leader reached into his pocket and fumbled around for a moment before pulling out a whistle with a small chain around it. He paused to take a long guzzle of his brew, broke the empty bottle against a rock and then leaned down face to face with the boy.

"Now, here's the whistle," the leader said sarcastically as he wrapped the whistle around the boy's neck. "This is your only other chance. When we walk away from here, if you fuckin' pussy out, you'd better blow this goddamn whistle before we're too far away to hear it. We hear the whistle, we come untie you, take you home, and we never wanna see you again. If not. . .hope we see you in the morning." He laughed again, then rammed the whistle in the boy's mouth.

"Now don't sneeze and blow that whistle out of your mouth, lessen you can put it back with your toes."

The whole group cackled. The leader waved his hand wildly, and the whole group scattered out of the clearing into the woods, several of them stumbling and laughing out of sight.

"Lets go, guys."

Zach and Jimmy hurdled a small bush and dropped to the ground behind its cover. Curry clumsily followed, falling hard to the dirt accidentally. He instantly raised his head to pour another half-bottle of brew inside. They all lay silently on the ground while they caught their breath. With the flashlights out now, only the moonlight lit the clearing. The rest of the guys were scattered about through the woods. Though the plan had called for everyone to watch from the outskirts of the field, most were so drunk that they forsook the plan in favor of the closest alcohol to be had. Only a few were still scattered in the bushes about 50 yards from the pledge tied to the tree.

Curry raised his head to peek over the bush at the boy. With his vision blurring, he peered for quite a period before focusing in on the moonlit shirt of the boy. He was fidgeting about with the awkward positioning he had been placed in. The whistle, still in his mouth, reflected an occasional beam out of the darkness.

"He's already trying to get loose," Curry snickered to Zach and Jimmy.

"Not so loud, man!" Jimmy whispered harshly to him.

"Fuck you, too," Curry snarled back. The alcohol always aided in agitating his already erratic personality.

"SHUSH," Zach interrupted.

They both glared at him for intruding, but dismissed it with another drink. All three raised their heads to see what was happening. The pledge was leaning against the tree, trying to push himself up with his legs. The loose parched soil gave no traction though, and he slipped to the ground, landing hard on his butt. The whistle popped out of his mouth, bouncing onto his chest.

"Shit," he grunted under his breath.

All three dropped to the ground, covering their mouths, attempting to cover an outburst of hysterical laughter. The boy didn't hear them though, due to his own scuffling making so much noise.

As they watched, the boy attempted to free himself over and over again. He tried standing again with the same result. Then he wiggled his hands, trying to squeeze them out of the tight loops. This was too painful, as it irritated the cuts on his wrists tremendously.

He was moving side to side when a flash caught his attention. It was a jagged piece of glass from one of the broken beer bottles. His leg stretched out to try and drag it over. After several attempts, he hooked it and scooted it across the dirt towards him. The boys, watching from a distance, frowned. This didn't fit into the plan. He's not supposed to get loose; it'll fuck everything up. Their hearts raced as their plan was unraveling. The glass was beside his thigh now. His legs weren't able to push it any further because of the strange position he sat in, so he started pushing sideways. He was trying to slide around the tree to reach it with his hands.

"That prick," Curry muttered as he lunged forward. His unstable reasoning got the best of him. He was furious at the thought of his plans being ruined. How dare the little bastard do that.

Zach grabbed him.

"What'd ya expect him to do?" Zach tried to reason. "He's supposed to be getting loose."

"He's supposed to try, not do it," Curry answered shakily.

"Give it a sec, man. He's not loose yet!"

They watched intently. The pledge slid around. His hands stretched blindly out to the glass. Their eyes strained to see if he reached it or not. The boy groaned as he stretched to his limit.

"DAMN!" he yelled, finally giving up.

That was the confirmation the boys needed. They sighed in relief as their heads dropped.

"We better not wait any longer," Curry announced to Zach and Jimmy.

"Yeah. . .you're right," they echoed.

"Did you get your dad's gun, Zach?" asked Curry.

Zach's face showed his concern. Curry asked him to take the gun as a precaution. It had been easily sneaked past his dad, who rarely saw it and surely wouldn't notice its absence. But he was still uneasy with it. What could they possibly need with a gun?

"Didn't you get it, Zach?"

"Yeah. . .I got it. I don't know what the big deal is. Why do we need a gun?"

"You never know. Ya gotta be ready for the worst. There's a lotta crazy people out there, Zach; I'm not gonna get caught off guard out here in the woods."

Curry, in all his drunkenness, thought this was a very reasonable explanation. Zach wondered though. It seemed a bit extreme to him. He had nothing against guns. He had been shooting occasionally, but a bunch of drunk college kids with a .38 caliber seemed ludicrous.

In his defense, Curry's attitudes weren't necessarily all his own idea. He'd grown up without his mom. His dad had fought in the jungles of Vietnam. Several years of this war life left permanent scars. And, unfortunately, it seemed that those scars were being passed along to Curry.

"Let's get back a little further while we get ready," Curry whispered, perfectly calm.

The three boys scurried away on all fours, like monkeys running through a thick jungle. The pledge caught this with his ears and jerked back around the tree to his original position. He peered into the trees in the general direction of the light noise. . .nothing. What was that? He wondered what the noise might be. But it was already gone, silent again except for the night bugs, crickets, frogs and such. His heart pounded fast in his bony chest. A certain paranoia was beginning to set in. So far, he wasn't even close to getting loose from the binding ropes. And the night noises seemed louder with the total silence that surrounded him. Sweat poured down his face even though a brisk cool breeze was steadily blowing. He shook his head hard, trying to blow the salty sweat out of his eyes, but they burned as it trickled into them anyway. So he tried to wipe them on his shoulder but couldn't reach.

The pledge heard another noise. His eyes blinked rapidly, washing the sweat so he could focus. The noise was getting louder, getting closer. His breathing got quicker with each rustling noise. It seemed to echo with his over-sensitive hearing. The anxiety drove him further over the edge. He looked at the whistle longingly.

"Hello? Anyone there?" he said nervously. The rustling seemed to subside slightly, but still intermittent, letting him know that someone or something was there. "Is anyone out there? C'mon guys. . .Is that you?"

Curry crept a few steps closer, followed by Jimmy to one side and then Zach behind him. They stayed back further from the clearing than before, over 100 yards from the pledge. Curry stood away from the other two boys for a reason. He held in his right hand a pair of leather leashes holding two huge dogs at bay. The dogs belonged to his father. They were just another of the odd things in Curry's life. Curry's dad trained attack dogs for use as watchdogs for businesses. It seemed everything around Curry related to violence in one way or another. This was no exception.

These dogs would surely intimidate any would-be burglar. They were both Doberman pinschers, but to the extreme as usual, these were not normal ones. These were a special breed of Doberman known as a warlock stock. They looked like a Doberman but were nearly twice the size, standing nearly a foot taller and 40 pounds heavier. The animals were a frightening presence, pulling on the two heavy leather leashes. Their heads bobbed from side to side, surveying the surroundings, while they panted heavily with the choker collars constricted tightly around the huge necks. Bright clean fangs glistened of saliva in the moonlight.

Curry had trouble holding the beasts back, especially while trying to stay low so as not to be spotted. He looked to his accomplices while wearing a large grin.

"Look at him," he whispered, pointing to the clearing. "He's scared as shit already."

Zach and Jimmy looked each other in the eye and then Curry.

"What. . .what is it?" Curry demanded. Even in this drunken state, he could read the obvious concern in both their eyes.

"I don't know about this, Curry," Zach spoke up.

"About what. . ."

"The dogs," he gestured. "Is this safe? Can we trust the dogs?"

"They'll be tied back, Zach. . .God, man, give it a rest!"

"Man, you better make sure they're tied good," Jimmy added. "If they get. . ."

"I'm not stupid, Jimbo," Curry interrupted.

"Okay..okay," they both echoed, retreating from a potential argument.

The dogs were well–trained. They sat alert while the three boys peered into the clearing. It was harder to see from this distance. The pledge was very jumpy and jerked his head with every sound he heard. They watched as he finally managed to stand. His movement was very restricted though, with his arms tied around the tree.

"We can't wait any more. Let's do it," Curry announced.

Jimmy nodded in agreement while Zach continued to watch the pledge.

"You got the rope?" Curry asked them.

"I got it," Jimmy answered, pulling a long nylon rope from a plastic bag and handing it to him.

Curry looked at it in his hand for a long time.

"What's wrong?" Jimmy asked.

"Nothin."

"What is it, Curry? Is it the wrong kinda rope? The wrong size? You didn't say what kinda rope to get, man."

"I said NOTHIN," Curry answered again sternly. "The rope's fine."

The rope wasn't fine though. It was way too thin. He looked at the wrapper as he went over to a tree about 10 yards closer. It was only 1/4 inch thick. His eyes moved over to the dogs. This rope could easily break under the stress of over 200 pounds of muscle, tugging relentlessly.

Oh well. Curry took a long drink of his beer, emptying it. He set the bottle down easily so no sound would find the pledge's ears. Reaching into his pocket, Curry pulled a huge hunting knife. Once again, the 7" blade seemed a bit overzealous.

Curry frowned to himself. He hadn't come this far to back down now. To quit now would screw up the whole evening. It wasn't his fault some idiot got this little rope. *'It probably won't break anyway,'* he told himself. *'And who cares if it does.'* The dogs were well–trained. They would listen to his commands.

He swung the measly rope around a tree and expertly tied a knot in that end. The rope was 250 feet, so Curry guessed and cut roughly 25 feet off. With the frayed end, he threaded and tied a knot through the two loops in the ends of the leashes. The two four-legged monsters watched with a cold nonchalant lack of interest. They remained at attention except for an occasional muscle twitch.

"Are you guys ready?" Curry whispered to the other two.

They nodded and looked back to the clearing where the pledge had worn himself down again and was panting heavily.

Curry pulled a white T-shirt from the inside pocket of his satin jacket. It belonged to the young boy tied around the tree. He crawled over in front of the dogs as their dark eyes followed him. Then he took the shirt and began rubbing it in one dog's face, then the other's. Both animals began to grow agitated and growl at the shirt.

The pledge perked up suddenly. The faint growl was loud enough to catch his attention. He peered into the darkness, trying to determine the general direction of the sounds.

"Hello. . .Is anyone there?" he asked timidly.

Zach and Jimmy ducked their heads grinning and used the opportunity to finish their beers. Meanwhile, a huge smile covered Curry's face as he continued to infuriate the dogs. He could barely keep from bursting into uncontrolled laughter and giving the whole thing away.

The dogs seemed as savage as hungry coyotes in the dead of winter. Continuing the effort, Curry slung the shirt in their faces as they snapped at it, their jaws popping shut. They growled thunderously and began barking as they leapt to their feet, no longer able to restrain themselves. Finally, Curry waved the shirt one more time, turning and pointing to the pledge and commanded the dogs to attack. They lunged forward barking brazenly as they trod away at a slow and confident pace.

Zach watched the thin white rope uncurl in front of his eyes. He worried that it was a bad idea, but in his drunken state, it wasn't a major concern. Only moments later the rope was close to being drawn taut. He stood up to see the dogs and pledge, to enjoy the show. The pledge was screaming at the top of his lungs. Zach hadn't even noticed until now. The fear was evident in his face.

All three boys raced forward. Their noise was covered by the barking dogs. Closer, they ducked behind some foliage, to one side of the field, where they could see everything.

As the dogs got closer to sniffing out their victim, their pace quickened. They were getting anxious now. Their noses told them that prey was near. Finally, to the three boys' delight, they emerged at a full run into the field. It was difficult to see with only the moonlight.

Curry began to laugh. That kid probably just shit his pants. If he figured it right the rope would snap tight only yards before the beasts reached their target. The others had not known how close Curry intended it to be. Zach's eyes widened while the dogs bolted toward the young man tied around the tree. Jimmy frowned, thinking something had gone wrong. But Curry only laughed louder.

If not for his panicked state, the pledge would surely have heard him. And he was definitely panicked. His terror was unimaginable. To him, these animals might have been hungry and rabid wolves. His only clues were the ferocious barking and the rustling they made through the woods. Even now, he had only just gotten a glimpse of the threatening animals.

Rational thinking was no longer an option. Instinctive thoughts of survival filled his head. It's amazing how many thoughts can race through one's mind in a desperate moment. *'Will they attack me? Most likely. Could the animals be intimidated into dismissing their intentions? Probably not! How long can I fight them off? How bad will they hurt me? Will they kill me? Will they leave me to bleed to death in agony? Will they eat me? Will they. . .will they. . .'* All this in the instant they entered the clearing and raced toward him.

Finally, at the last possible moment, the rope pulled taut, snapping the angry dogs back only a few feet away. The force of the snap sent both dogs to the ground as their necks stopped instantly, while swinging their hind ends around in a circle. They yelped loudly as they fell to the ground. Undaunted though, both jumped back to their feet, leaping into the air at the rope's end, still trying desperately to reach the boy.

He screamed in terror and turned away. But they didn't attack him. Why? He turned back slowly to face them. They lunged wildly toward him, from about 10 feet away. But, luckily, they were still no closer. Both animals were snarling, saliva drooling from their jaws of bared teeth.

At last the pledge realized they still wanted to get to him desperately, they just couldn't reach him. Something held them at bay. He looked closer at the huge animals. They had collars on. . .and leashes. He followed the leather back to the hand loop a few feet back. Here he finally noticed the white rope. It was barely even dirty yet. The moon's light reflected fairly brightly off of it.

It was a trick. He was set up for the enjoyment of the frat brothers. He tried to breathe a sigh of relief, but as of yet was still too frightened to calm down. The dogs barked relentlessly, and the background remained silent except for one lone noise. It grew louder and more distinct: Curry's laughter. Zach and Jimmy snickered along with him. The rope wasn't too long. Everything was okay. They were drunk. They were amused.

"HEY," the pledge yelled over the dogs. "Who's there?"

Curry's laughter only grew stronger.

"WHO'S THERE?" he demanded unamused by the entire stunt.

Instantly, Curry was silent. He stood straight up revealing himself to the boy. The other twos' chuckling trailed off. Curry wasn't amused any longer, either. Zach and Jimmy looked at each other realizing that the pledge may have just provoked Curry into an outburst. He had a short fuse, especially when drinking.

"Sinbad. . .Damion!" Curry called to the dogs. "Stop. Sit. . .Stay!"

The dogs amazingly stopped their pursuit and immediately sat down. They were still anxious, though. And they peered hatefully through the boy tied to the tree, still growling lightly.

Curry stepped from behind the bush, walking quickly to confront the boy up close. Zach and Jimmy stood warily and followed him into the clearing. Curry stopped beside the dogs while the other two stayed back a bit. They seemed to be the only ones there. The others were supposed to be hidden around the perimeter of the field. No one else came forward. Zach wondered if they had lost interest and went after more beer or just passed out in the woods.

"HEY, BOY! YOU GOT A PROBLEM?" Curry yelled.

"This is bullshit, man," the pledge called back. "Who the hell you think you are, Curry?"

Curry's blood was already starting to boil. His glassy bloodshot eyes stared as deeply as the two dogs beside him.

"I'm the one who decides if you're in or not, you little shit," he screamed. "So don't mouth me!"

"I don't wanna be in your damn frat man. . .You're a lunatic!" The pledge was so upset he was fighting tears back. "Fuck you!"

With that remark, Curry bolted at the pledge. Zach leapt forward to stop him. When Curry reached the boy, he punched him in the gut, partially doubling him over. Then, with as much force as he could muster, he backhanded him across the jaw. Blood spewed from the boy's mouth. He coughed uncontrollably, trying to regain his breath. Before Curry could do more damage, Zach reached him, wrapping him up and pulling him off the boy.

"Get your damn hands off me," Curry screamed at Zach.

"Cool it, man!"

He pulled but couldn't escape Zach's grasp. In front of them, the pledge was crying freely.

"What's wrong, you fagot?" he taunted the boy.

"Cool it, man," Zach repeated. "We're gonna get in trouble if you don't calm down. . ."

"He's insane. . ." the pledge cried to Zach.

"Shut up," Zach insisted. He knew comments like this would only infuriate Curry more.

"Yeah, that's right, shut up," Curry chimed in.

"You okay?" Zach asked Curry.

"Yeah. . .I'm fine," he answered.

"Okay. I'm letting you go. Don't start up again. . . okay?"

"I won't. The prick's not worth it." He looked back at the pledge. "You fuckin' mama's boy!"

Zach slowly removed his arms from around Curry who straightened his jacket, while giving out a dirty look to the pledge.

"Don't do it!" Zach repeated to Curry, anticipating his thoughts.

"You're right, Zach," Curry replied. "Screw him."

Curry turned his back to the pledge and slowly walked away. Zach stayed beside him, close enough to restrain him if he changed his mind. Curry walked back to where the dogs still anxiously sat. Zach looked over at Jimmy, who was still standing in the background, getting more concerned by the minute, when suddenly Curry reached into his pocket, pulling out the T-shirt from earlier. He threw it to the ground in front of the dogs.

"ATTACK!" he yelled to them, pointing at the pledge.

The dogs bolted from their sitting position in a mass of growling and barking. Zach jumped back as they surprised him. Jimmy did the same, stumbling backward and almost falling to the ground.

"Shit," Jimmy said.

The pledge jerked back and turned his head instinctively to avoid the dogs even though he knew they were bound.

Curry burst into laughter. He stepped to the side away from the dogs a few feet. They were as vicious as before, needing desperately to reach that boy tied to that tree. Their frustration grew worse as they leapt forward over and over again, only to be yanked to the ground by the frail rope looped through the lead straps of their leashes. Unable to reach their prey, they began to snap at each other instead.

"Stop it. . .Please!" exclaimed the helpless boy, who was squirming against the tree.

"Go to hell!" Curry snarled back at him.

"Call'em off, Curry," Zach yelled.

Curry gave Zach a challenging look.

The dogs lunged forward. In desperation, they started fighting with one another. Both animals jerked back and forth wildly, while trying to grab each others' throats, an instinctive move from deep within. Finally, there was no more holding back their fury. The rope snapped. The beasts rolled forward to only a few feet from the pledge.

"Oh shit!" Jimmy yelled. "They're loose!" He turned and ran into the darkness in pure terror.

Zach and Curry both stumbled backward a few feet. They watched in horror as the dogs tumbled around biting each other in a furious battle.

"Sinbad. Damion. Stop!" Curry commanded.

The four-legged monsters were out of control, though. His voice didn't even phase their aggression. In the midst of the fight, they rolled again, even closer to the helpless pledge.

"Do something!" Zach yelled.

They rolled one more time and one hit the boy. It instinctively turned its head and snapped at him. The other now realized it could reach him also and abandoned its attack on its brother. The first one sunk its teeth deep into the boy's calf. Blood instantly soaked through his blue jeans, and he cried out in pain. The second followed its ears, lunging for the source of the noise. The boy snapped his head back. Its jaws clamped shut only inches from his face, while the back of his head slammed hard into the tree trunk that was holding him.

Curry stood frozen, dazed by the scene in front of him. He said nothing. He seemed unsure of it, unsure of stopping it. After all, this guy shouldn't get away with that disrespect. Who does he think he is?

"What do we do?" Zach ran over to Curry and turned him to his face. "Snap out of it. We gotta help him."

"Okay. . .You're right." Curry responded.

Zach thought he seemed reluctant or at least slow to react, but in that same split second, his mind raced back to the pledge.

Curry called the dogs again. They ignored him. The pledge desperately kicked at the beasts with his good leg. The other was in excruciating pain from the wound to his calf. He screamed pitifully for help.

The first dog grabbed his still foot, which was already wet with the blood from the bite above. It yanked back and forth, not wanting to let loose. The foot was being mutilated, shaken like a rag doll being playfully ripped from the hands of a master teasing its pet. The second jumped into the air again, not content with the lower portion of his body as the other dog was. The pledge twisted sideways trying to avoid the incoming dog. It hit him with the force of a sledgehammer and sunk its teeth deep into his skinny upper arm. He screamed again. The pain was unimaginable. And the dog didn't let go, either. With both its weight and muscle, it pulled downward on his arm as though trying to rip it from its body. The flesh and muscle tore raggedly while blood sprayed instantly into the air and onto the boy's face. Finally, the dog slipped back to the ground. Huge hunks of skin hung like spaghetti noodles from his arm. Both dogs tasted blood and weren't about to quit now.

Zach was horrified.

"The gun!" Curry yelled. "Zach, use the gun."

Zach reached into the back of his pants and pulled the weapon from his waist. It was a plain and simple pistol, nothing elaborate, just a short barreled .38 with the blue finish, slightly dulled. Was this the only choice though?

"I can't," he yelled back to Curry with his eyes fixed on the gun in his hand. "What if I hit him?"

"It's your only choice. . .Shoot the dogs. . .You can do it." The whole time Curry backed slowly away as if distancing himself from the setting.

Zach raised the gun and fired into the air. A flash of fire blew from the barrel a foot into the air. But they continued, undaunted. His last resort was to shoot them. He lowered the gun into position. Looking down the barrel, his eyes were focused on the sights, then refocused on the target, allowing the sights to blur slightly. He could hardly see in the dim moonlight. Or was it the beer? He realized how frightened he actually was. His hands would not steady. They were shaking fiercely.

"Shoot man, SHOOT," Curry screamed, running up to Zach.

Zach was frozen.

"DO IT!!!" he yelled into his ear.

Suddenly, amidst the violent shaking of his hands, the gun went off. A flash lit the field for an instant. The dogs scattered away from the boy and into the woods. Zach was temporarily blinded by the flash and couldn't tell what happened.

Instantly the woods were silent. Then Zachery heard something. He took a few steps toward the tree to see the outcome. The noise was the body of the pledge sliding down the tree trunk and slowly slumping to the ground.

"Oh God." Zach dropped the gun into the dirt in front of his feet.

Curry walked up to the body coldly. He didn't seem shaken by the sight, instead pushing the body back by the shoulders and leaning it against the tree. The bullet had struck the middle of his chest, completely missing the dog. Zach turned away and got sick.

"You shot him," Curry accused Zach as he walked over to him.

"You told me to shoot, man," Zach defended.

"I didn't tell you to shoot HIM. Shoot the dogs!"

"For Christ's sake, I didn't do it on purpose. It was an accident, Curry."

"I thought you knew how to use a gun, Crawford!"

"I was scared, man. . ."

"I knew you couldn't be trusted with a gun," Curry preached. "I should've taken it."

"Will you shut up about the gun? We gotta do something."

"Like what?"

"We gotta call the cops, man. . .We gotta get to a phone. . .Come on, let's go."

"Like HELL! I'm not goin' to jail because you shot some kid, Crawford."

"We won't go to jail. . .It was an accident. . .We'll tell 'em what happened. . .Tell 'em the whole thing."

"Zachery." Curry grabbed his chin and turned him back to face the limp body. "When they see him tied to that tree, they ain't gonna believe you. They'll think the whole thing was premeditated. I'm not gonna cover for you if you run to the cops about this."

Curry waved his hands wildly, emphasizing his point. . . I'm absolved of the whole thing if you do that.

"What do we do then?" Zach couldn't think straight. He was on the edge of going into shock. Nothing made sense. He felt sobered up, but was he really? Should he listen to Curry?

"We gotta get rid of the body!" Curry commanded.

"What?"

"You heard me. Nobody will ever find out if we stick together." Curry was trying to manipulate Zach. "I'll help ya, Zach. Just stick with me, and you ain't gonna get caught."

"It's not right though, Curry! We have to tell someone."

"If you tell anyone, WE'LL BOTH GO TO JAIL. . .And I'm not even the one that shot him. . .They won't believe you anyway!"

Zach paced the ground, only inches from where the gun still lay. He had shot someone. His life was ruined. His future was over. So many plans. So many dreams. What if the authorities didn't believe him, as Curry suggested? Everyone would think he was a cold-blooded killer. Not only that, with the way the crime scene looked, he would be branded insane. He tied a boy up, tortured him, then shot him straight in the chest. Maybe Curry was right. Maybe they should hide the body. They were the only ones that knew. Not even Jimmy knew. He ran when the dogs got loose. He didn't see the rest of the horrible event.

"What's it gonna be, man?" Curry's voice pushed back into his consciousness. It was noticeably subdued, compared to a few moments ago.

"I don't know. . ."

"We gotta do it, Zach. . .It's the only choice. . .Come'on, I'll help, don't worry."

Curry patted Zach's back encouragingly.

"Okay. . .I guess maybe you're right. . .Maybe. . ." Zach trailed off.

They cut the body loose. Zach remembered the bloody wrists from earlier in the evening. It barely looked like a scratch compared to the rest of the body, which slumped over to the ground without the rope and tree trunk holding it up.

Curry went to the feet, motioning for Zach to get the arms and shoulders so they could carry it out of the opening. Zach took a deep breath and reached under the arms. The right arm had been mutilated by the dog. Zach dropped the body and stumbled to the ground throwing up again. Tears began pouring down his face. Curry stood behind him, his expression indifferent while Zachery bawled like a hungry baby.

"Pull yourself together, man," Curry demanded. "It's gonna be daylight soon."

A faint hint of light was beginning to show on the eastern horizon. Zach wiped the tears from his face and got back up to his feet, trying to get hold of himself. They carried the body several hundred yards into the woods. Then Curry sent Zach to his truck for a shovel while he gathered up the rope and anything else incriminating.

Zach began digging. Curry watched for a very long time before finally offering to take a turn. Zach didn't want the help, though. He couldn't sit still next to that body. He kept digging. The sun rose brightly into the sky, a beautiful day. A beautiful day for a burial? Sweat rolled from Zach's face, a stench of alcohol permeating from it. His head throbbed. But he continued to work as hard as possible until he collapsed, gasping for air. Thirty seconds later he started again where he had left off. A grave was not an easy hole to dig. And leaving the young man here in the ground wasn't an easy thing to live with. He wiped his face with his forearm, while trying to catch his breath, wishing the horrible thoughts would leave his mind.

"That's deep enough," Curry blurted out.

"You think so?" Zach was so unnerved that he still wasn't thinking about this whole thing, about what he was doing.

"Yes," Curry answered disgustedly. He was worn thin with his own hangover. The hot sun wasn't helping, and he was quickly losing his patience and interest. He seemed unmoved by this terrible tragedy, caring only about getting back home. "Come on."

They pulled the body over to the hole. It seemed so heavy. Curry grabbed around the ankles hastily, anxious to deposit it into its grave. Zach was looking at him, breathing heavily, and trying to avoid eyeing the body. Curry nodded at him to grab the other side. He leaned down and reached his hands under the boy's armpits. His eyes still stared forward. The skin was clammy and sticky with drying blood. Zach felt his stomach rolling again, and released the body, allowing it to drop back to the dirt as he turned and vomited again. Nothing was left in his belly though, as he heaved wildly.

"Straighten up, Crawford!"

Zach held up his hand to stall Curry for a moment.

He turned back to the body and picked it up again. This time he noticed the gritty feel of dirt sticking to the poor boy's bloody arms. In a quick motion they swung it into the shallow hole. It landed with a thud and its limbs twisted unnaturally. Zach lost his balance and nearly fell into the hole on top of the boy. A chill ran up his spine as a bead of sweat ran down it.   All the while, Curry snickered at the frightened look that came over Zachery's face.

"You ready?" Curry asked, while picking up the shovel. "We can't waste any more time.   Everyone'll wonder where we are."

"Yeah," Zach answered as tears began streaming down his face yet another time.

Curry reached the shovel out to him, and Zach took it from his outstretched hand.   Tears dripped from his face. He swooped the shovel into the loose dirt beside the makeshift grave.   Slowly he turned to the grave and turned the shovel over, letting the first load fall directly onto the chest and pale face.

"OH, GOD," Zachery Crawford cried out.   "PLEASE FORGIVE ME. . .I'M SORRY, GOD. . .PLEASE, GOD. . ."

Chapter
Seventeen

Zach jumped up. He was lying in bed. Sweat poured from his forehead, and his breathing was strained again. Disgusted, he swung his feet to the floor, burying his face in the palms of his hands. The dream again. It seemed more vivid than ever. The time was only 1:00 A.M., and he had already been awakened by his terrible memory of that night. Although, with all that'd been going on, it was surprising he managed to fall asleep at all.

He thought of Curry. He'd be surprised if the memory ever haunted HIM. Oh. . .He realized the truth. Soon after that night Zach realized that it wasn't totally his fault. Curry had set the scene. Curry unnecessarily set into motion the events that led to the boy's death. Curry was just covering his own ass that night. They did what they did though. . .no denying it. They hid the body. It was never found. They were never accused of any crime, and Zachery had been trying to live with himself ever since. Despite this enlightened view of that night, Zach was still painfully aware that he had shot a young man. For that, he could never forgive himself.

He roamed his apartment aimlessly as he worried about the predicament he was in. The dream had scared him wide awake as usual. When was it all going to end? The world was crumbling around him, and all he could do was watch.

He may not be able to confront Curry, but he could sure as hell do something, right or wrong. It was time to find out who was behind the computer break-ins at Global, once and for all.

He slowly rolled to a stop on a dark side street, across the intersection and back a short distance from his employer's offices. He was clothed in blue jeans and a dark shirt and shoes. It was time. The hour was late enough that the guards should be settled in for awhile. It was all rather melodramatic, he thought to himself, but he didn't know of any other way to do it.

The information he needed was there in the computer, but he would have to extract it from the main terminals in the computer room. Afraid that the intruder might find it himself, Zach had hidden the files from any outside access, and it was too busy during the day. He'd tried several times, only to be interrupted by a co-worker taking an interest in what he was doing. He couldn't let anyone else know. . .they'd probably think that he was crazy anyway, and after all, he wasn't so sure if they would be wrong. This way he could sneak in, see what he needed to see, and then sneak back out without anyone else's knowing. Or, at least, that was the plan.

He quietly exited the car, leaving it parked in the dark alley and walking the block or so to the building complex. As he approached the grounds, he stopped and kneeled down to survey closely for anyone in the parking lot. It seemed to be empty from his vantage point. His attention turned to the front gates, which were closest and easiest to reach but much too well lit. He couldn't risk being seen in the light, so he looked down the fence line to the far side of the complex where there was another gate. It looked fairly dark, so Zachery decided to use that entrance. He took another quick glance, then started off in a full run towards the gates. When he reached them, he paused for a few moments to catch his breath. Until now, he'd never appreciated how big the complex was, having never walked around the grounds. It was really quite large, probably 150 yards between the two gates, and there was another set of gates on the other side.

Zach pulled a ring of keys from his pocket, grasping them tightly to keep them from jingling and making noise. He held the keys up in the air so that he could make out their silhouettes against the moonlight. This was one thing that would make it easier tonight. He'd always been entrusted with a full set of keys to all the locks in the building, except for those on the top floor, that is.

He unlocked the gate and swung it open, just enough to slip through. It squealed somewhat, causing Zach to wince at the noise. He sidestepped through the opening and dropped to the ground surveying the empty lot. Still no one around. He closed the gate behind him taking great care to avoid the squeal this time, then locked it again. It was a chance he had to take in case one of the guards walked around the lot. An open or unlocked gate would most certainly be cause for a full search of the premises.

There was a small side door toward the corner of the building, far away from the main entrance. Zach took another quick glance around, then broke into a sprint across the parking lot towards the building. His heart pounded thunderously in his ears as he darted toward the single door. He pulled the keys from his pocket again and used one to momentarily shut off the alarm so that he could quietly slip inside. Once inside, he quickly turned the alarm back on, hoping that the guard at the front desk hadn't noticed that it had been momentarily de-activated.

Zachery found himself at the end of a long, pitch dark hallway. He felt his way along the block walls until he reached the end of the corridor, his eyes still trying to adjust to the darkness. A very faint squeak emanated from the floor with each step Zach took with his rubber–soled shoes. At the end of the hall he peeked around the corner, unsure just exactly where he was. A dim EXIT sign shed red light down this hall.

Then, from nowhere, a man walked across the corridor that Zach was looking down. He abruptly pulled his head back, banging it on the concrete block wall behind him. A flash of white filled his vision as instant throbbing filled his head. It hurt like hell, but he didn't dare make a noise. He was so scared that he didn't even dare to breathe, though his heart was pounding so hard he felt sure the man could hear it. The few seconds that the guard took to pass seemed like an eternity. He finally let out a deep sigh and breathed in deeply to provide the oxygen his lungs craved. Slowly, he made his way down the hall to the lighted one where he peaked his head around another corner ever so slightly. Realizing where he was, Zach dashed across that hall and through a fire escape door.

He stopped again for just a minute to listen for any noise. Still believing that he was breathing too heavily, he held his breath to listen again. Even the silence was loud. He strained more but still heard nothing. It was time to move on.

It had taken almost thirty minutes to get this far. Paranoid about getting caught, he decided to quicken his pace. He started up the stairs at a full run, taking two steps at a time. When he reached the floor that the computer room was on, Zachery stopped again to catch his breath and peer through the small window in the door. He was breathing heavily, and sweat dripped from his body while his hot breath steamed up the window. He felt as if his whole body were on fire. As frightened as he was, his blood pressure must have skyrocketed, but he had to move on.

The hall was empty, but Zachery could still see the slow movements of the cameras which protected that entrance into the computer room. If he moved at the right time, he could run across the hall and under one, then into the computer room at the time they swung away from the doors. He watched the cameras swinging back and forth for what seemed to be an eternity. The move had to be at precisely the right moment. He had to be sure that the timing was down, that he didn't move too soon or too late. Finally, at the precise time, he lunged across the brightly lit hallway to the other side and slid across the hall until he was under the camera. As he lay there, the stairway exit door clicked shut. When the latch caught, it seemed as if it must have echoed through the entire building.

He keyed a special code into the locking mechanism on the computer room door, a little present to himself. He had put this secret code into the security system earlier, suspecting that his assigned code wouldn't work again as had happened the time before when he tried to get in after hours. The door popped open immediately, and he tiptoed through it and then the second door into the computer room, closing it behind him.

The darkness hit him hard, and he opened his eyes wide, darting them quickly back and forth in an effort to adjust. The many small lights from the computer system were lit and flashing throughout the room, as usual. It gave Zach a false sense of security. He pulled a small, pocket flashlight from his hip pocket and shined it towards the main terminals. Almost there. He knew how close he was to finding the answers to his questions as he kneeled down in front of the main terminal, pushing the chair aside in case he had to move quickly.

As he started typing, his fingers moved freely over the keyboard. He called into memory the data files that he had hidden in the computer's memory. He had protected them so that they could only be accessed from a special program he wrote. He scanned through page after page of seemingly garbled, meaningless information. The bits and pieces of work the intruder had done were being stored not just in his intended location, but here also, as he sent them through the network to the main computer. Zach had always been good with communications, and this was where the traps were hidden. Scanning the data, he recognized the programs, but not the specific routines placed into them. Zachery scribbled notes down on a piece of paper, shoving it down into his pocket. He thought he knew what it meant but decided to follow it through before doing anything drastic. He wished he could print this out on paper but didn't dare make that much noise. He knew the guards patrolled routinely.

He continued his reading and searching of the file. The heavy perspiration had nearly stopped, but his heart still pounded as the adrenaline flowed through his body. His hands were getting shaky, and his palms were wet and clammy, movements becoming erratic as he was more and more frightened with every word his eyes passed over.

Suddenly, the door knob began turning and the door opened. Zach hit the floor instantly, sliding a few feet up against the disk drive cabinets to hide himself. Out of the corner of his eye, Zach noticed something, the computer was still rolling up words on the terminal from his last command. One of two guards had now stepped into the room. He stood just inside the door, shining a light around. His silhouette cast a long shadow across the clean white tile. Neither was the guard that had confronted him that day . . . Cavanaugh. Zach figured he was caught, cornered like a mouse.

"Hey, what's this?"

Zachery looked, and sure enough the guard was shining the flashlight on the moving words.

"What is it?" the other asked disgustedly.

"Look, this computer's doing something."

They both took a couple steps forward. They were still a safe distance away as Zach positioned himself to run in case he was discovered. He felt as though even his breathing was loud, so he tried to hold his breath, only taking shaky faint erratic breaths while he strained to listen.

Both guards watched for a few seconds.

"Hey, man," started the one that had stayed further back. "What if that thing's screwing up?"

"I don't know. . .think we should call someone?"

"Hell no, I think we should get out of here!"

"Why?"

"Cause we're gonna get blamed for messing this thing up. It's probably worth over a million dollars!"

"Oh, bull shit!"

"Bull shit, my ass! Let's get out of here." They both shined their lights quickly around the room. They weren't really looking for anything, just making their rounds. Then they turned and walked out, pulling the door closed behind them. Zach collapsed to the floor with a sigh with relief.

But there was no time to relax. Since he couldn't make a print-out of what he'd found, Zachery decided to copy everything to a portable disk to take home with him for safe keeping. As he sat in the silence and darkness of the room, waiting for the copy to finish, his thoughts began to wander to Taylor and what was going to come of their relationship. He desperately loved her. She was everything he could ask for. His life had been so empty before she entered it, and he'd never even realized it. Bob had always been right. It was their love that kept him going throughout this ordeal, giving him the strength to face each day.

Her beauty was indescribable: more beautiful than the most wonderful summer day on a tropical island, more beautiful than a fresh snowfall in the Appalachian Mountains. Her love had been undaunting in this ordeal, and he knew that she'd endured a lot. She treated him like a king, handled him as a . . ..

Luckily a noise broke his train of thought. He ran over to the window, sliding up against the wall beside it. His fingers pulled the curtain open very slowly, just enough to see out. Two dark colored sedans were speeding through the parking lots towards the front entrance. They screeched to a stop, and two men in suits got out of each car. A third man exited one of the sedans a moment later. It looked like Cavanaugh. As the security guard ran out to meet them, a cold chill ran up Zach's spine all the way into his neck. He was completely confused. If the two guards had seen him, they would have said so then. After all, there were two of them, and they did carry guns. He glanced across the room to the computer; it was still copying. Then he noticed the camera in the corner. He had believed there was no monitor, that it was fake. But did it actually work, just like the ones in the hallway?

"Damn, hurry up," he whispered aloud, in an effort to prod the copy.

His attention turned back to the parking lot. The men were talking to two guards now, maybe the two that were just in here, Zachery thought. Both of them were shrugging their shoulders. Did this mean the two guards did or didn't know about him? Then several of the men reached into their coats and pulled out guns, and all broke into a run, heading toward the front entrance of the building.

'This is it!' he told himself. They were coming up after him. He ran to the computer, sliding to a stop in front of it.

"C'mon, c'mon, finish, you bitch!" he said as he pounded his fist on the table.

The lights stopped; it was done. A frantic Zach pulled the disk from its drive, and with the copy in hand, ran to the door. He opened it slowly, peeking up at the cameras. It would be better if they didn't see him leave, that way they wouldn't know which direction he'd gone. They were moving away from the stairs, so he sprinted towards the stairway door.

He started down the steps but heard a noise right away. Another door had slammed open, and they were on their way up. The footsteps echoed up through the stairwells, finding his ears. Zachery froze. He peeked over the rail a tiny bit and was surprised to see that they were actually within sight, their hands grasping the handrail as they took the steps, three at a time. He crawled to the landing below him and ducked into the hallway, hoping they would pass him. This floor was empty, with no guards on it, but it was only one floor below the computer room. He heard the footsteps getting closer now. It was at least three men running full speed up the stairs. Their hard-soled shoes clicked loudly on the metal plates at the edge of each step.

Suddenly it was silent as they reached the landing where Zach was hiding behind the door. He watched as the doorknob began turning only inches in front of his eyes.

"It's the next floor, sir," someone yelled.

At that, they started running the stairs to the next floor. Zach thought he heard the door open and close, so it was now or never. He slung the door open and broke into a run heading down the stairs, taking each half flight with two steps and slinging himself around the corners with his hand tightly on the banister. He couldn't afford to be careful now; there was too little time. He poked his head out the door back on the first floor, then ran into the dark hallway from which he had originally come. The darkness had practically blinded him, but he kept running full speed, hoping he didn't get lost. His fear drove him forward even harder.

He rounded the last corner before the door and suddenly ran straight into one of the guards, knocking them both to the floor. The guard's head hit very hard against the floor while Zachery landed on top of him, slightly cushioning his fall. They slid several feet on the freshly waxed flooring.

Zach grabbed his own forehead in pain, where their heads had butted as they collided. He jumped back up and went for the door, weaving into the wall as he took off. Looking over his shoulder, he saw that the guard was even more dazed than himself from the blow to his head and was getting up very slowly. Maybe he still had a chance to get away.

Finally he cracked the door open, then peeked out enough to scan the lot. It looked clear, so he slammed the door open and ran for his life. Forget the alarm, forget caution. It was do or die. The parking lot never seemed so big, the cool wind rushing into his ears as he sprinted. He was already tired and knew it was the adrenaline alone that kept him going. He fumbled for his keys at the gate, even dropping them on the blacktop. Maybe he shouldn't have locked it after all. Grabbing them up, Zach had to try three keys before finally finding the correct one.

He swung the gate wide open, went through and across the street where it was a little darker. He still had to go the width of the complex, without being spotted in order to reach his car on the other side. By now his lungs needed more oxygen than he could provide, as he gasped for air. He slowed down just a hair, to a fast jog, to try to catch his breath. But it was only for a moment.

"There he is!"

Zach turned his head only to see one of the guards yelling from across the street. Another was exiting the same door that he had used. He quickened the pace again, air or no air. Looking over his shoulder, he saw two men on foot and one running for a car. If he got to that car quick enough, it was all over. Finally, his own car was in sight. He fumbled for the keys in his jeans pocket again. *I'm gonna make it, I'm gonna make it!* he told himself, over and over.

When Zach got to the car, his hands were shaking so badly that he couldn't get the key into the keyhole. It kept bouncing around on the side of the door, missing the keyhole and nicking the expensive paint. After several desperate tries, he finally slid the key in and jerked it clockwise to unlock. He slammed the lock down as he closed the door behind him. The key easily slid into the ignition, and the foreign car fired up instantly as he twisted it.

The BMW roared loudly to life while Zach pushed the stick into first gear. It took off, throwing him back deep into the seat, and he pushed it hard before switching gears and running the two guards out of his way.

He was nearly free, and then from nowhere, one of the large sedans slid across his path, effectively blocking the intersection in front of him. Zach panicked for a quick second but immediately pulled himself back together. His left foot pushed the clutch into the floor, then he shifted down into a lower gear. He wasn't thinking straight now, just running on instinct. . .running for his life. With his left hand, he spun the wheel as hard as he could while pushing the accelerator to the floor and sidestepping the clutch. The rear tires screamed and smoke rolled from them as the car spun completely around in the middle of the road. But, instead of letting up, he pushed the car harder, practically standing on the gas pedal. The tachometer read well into the red zone before he jammed it into the next gear, heading away from the sedan now, with the rear end of his car still violently fishtailing back and forth. He kept pushing it though, slamming into the next gear and across the intersection before he could be blocked again. Even drawing a deep sigh of relief, Zach continued accelerating. He spotted an entrance to the freeway and slid across several lanes into the berm, almost missing the on-ramp.

'I'm safe for now,' he told himself, knowing that his car was fast enough to lose them. But he knew he couldn't go home. It certainly wouldn't be safe there. 'What to do? Think! Think!' He had to find somewhere safe, a safe haven, if only for a short time.

Chapter Eighteen

After he jumped up to the interstate and put some distance between him and his pursuers, Zachery drove to the outskirts of town. He hadn't realized just how far he had driven until he passed Great America. The amusement park had already opened its gates for the summer, but was dark and empty at 4:00 A.M., except for a lone pickup truck sweeping the monstrous parking lot. He found a small dumpy hotel to spend the remainder of the night in, after crossing into Wisconsin and making sure to park the car in a dark lot across from the hotel. It had to be out of sight from the road.

The surroundings were certainly not what Zach was accustomed to. The room smelled more like an animal shelter, and there were holes in the plaster of the thin walls. A couple argued in the next apartment. It seemed he had been flirting too much with her best friend at a party earlier that evening. She wasn't going to be humiliated like that again. . .blah, blah. The sheets were old and stained, with no covers on the pillows, unlike the slick satin sheets Zach slept between each night. The floor seemed as good a place as any to sit, as he lay his head back against the corner of the bed. He looked at the unswept carpet under the dresser. Something lay under it. Zach's best guess put it to be a well-aged french fry.

'How did they know?' he kept asking himself, tossing the computer disk around in his hand. The only answer that he could come up with was actually the correct one. They had their own private security system set up. Maybe the supposed fake cameras in the corners of the computer room weren't quite so fake after all. The guard station had no monitors showing the inside of the computer room, but what if the monitors did exist somewhere else. *'As big as this is I wouldn't be surprised. . .I wonder if they've taken it any further. Are we being watched? Maybe they bugged the offices, too.'*

Zach was right again, but he hadn't realized to what extent they had carried it. He never dreamed that his private life had also been invaded. But it was. The apartment too was under surveillance. But then, all key executives were being observed.

Could his life ever be the same? Knots formed in his stomach again. *'Why couldn't I have left it alone?'* he asked himself. *'Two months ago I had it all, a great job. . .lots of money, the respect of my peers. But maybe it was all a lie. Maybe I'm not who I think at all. Have they been playing me all along? Am I just the front to a big scam. . .hand-picked because I'm too stupid to figure it out, to catch them? I was making a small fortune, had everything I ever dreamed of, and now I'm going to lose it all, and, if I'm not careful, I'll lose my life, too. Why?'* he asked himself. *'Why?'*

An outburst of tears and sobbing came over Zach, but he quickly stopped, realizing he had to pull himself together if he was going to survive. Beating himself up wasn't the answer. He didn't know if it was their plan, but too bad if it was. It might have taken awhile, but he DID catch on. And now they would pay.

He wasn't sure what to do. However, it seemed obvious that he had to be sure of what he saw on that display in the computer room. Zach pulled his notebook computer from a case and hit the power switch, at the same time inserting the infamous computer disk. Was he right? Did he really see what he thought as the words flew by earlier. There was only one way to find out. And if so, then so be it, time to go to the police.

As he sat in the darkness, only the dull bluish light of the computer screen hit Zach's weary eyes. The disk, about seventy-five cents worth of plastic and metal, had done its job. Now it held the futures of many lives in its humble bits and bytes. No matter how many times he looked at the data, the answer was the same. He didn't want to believe it, but there was no denying the facts.

It looked like a typical money skimming operation. All this was over some crooks stealing money. This was state-of-the-art thievery, though electronic, not in person. No guns or getaway cars, only passwords and keystrokes. But it was theft, plain and simple, nothing more. It looked like the operation had been underway for a long time, with LakeShore being just another in a long string of corporate victims. Modifications were inserted into programs that were running these businesses. They were subtle changes that no one would notice, and things that couldn't be traced even if they were noticed. If found, they might appear to be program bugs, rather than deliberate.

Without the logs that Zach had created and copied to this disk, there was no chance of figuring out who did it, even if the changes were noticed. As scary as it seemed, the changes were very widespread, as though every conceivable calculation had been altered. Obviously it was a very delicate operation though, masterminded by someone with intimate knowledge of the project, not to mention a good understanding of the general methodologies used by the company within every project. Whoever was doing this knew when to strike, he knew to wait until the specific time that a program was successfully unit tested. This would be the point of hands off by any programming staff. Then the changes were made after the client was already satisfied and had accepted the program.

Everything was centered around numbers. Only the types of things that required complex complications were touched. For instance, a calculation to compound interest on savings accounts had been altered to shave a fraction of a percentage off, maybe a tenth of a percentage, and deposit it into a holding account. On a small account it would only be a couple pennies, but on a larger account maybe a couple dollars or more, small enough to be passed off as differences in rounding due to the computer processor's instruction set. Zach had certainly seen his share of that.

The same types of things had been done on loans. When the amortization schedules were done, a fraction was added to the monthly payment. Again, it would only be a small fraction from a few cents to a few dollars, depending on the size of the loan, and again it would be put into the holding account and passed off as rounding differences. These pennies and dollars don't seem like a lot, but multiply them by the thousands of customers with thousands of savings accounts and loans and consider the business customers with millions of dollars flowing through their accounts every day. Their contributions to the holding account ran into hundreds, even thousands of dollars a day.

The holding account was done brilliantly. For all intensive purposes, it was a blip. . .somewhere in memory. The account never existed from day to day, never showed on hard copy reports, but its dollars were always there to be included in balancing the ledgers or completing totals. Then, at the end of the day, the computer was set up to silently dial up and transfer this money into other accounts.

From the looks of the dial-up the computer was doing, it was probably an offshore account dialed overseas, but it still didn't answer the burning question. . .who?

Maybe he could find out by following the transfer account. It was a long shot, but that account number was the only information he had. With expert ease, Zach pressed the touchpad and double-clicked an icon to his modem. It responded with the ever familiar touch tone dialing, and he was instantly connected to his Internet provider. From there he could go anywhere.

Suddenly a quick flash appeared in the corner of his screen. He recognized it as nothing unusual, only email. He clicked it, out of habit, not even considering that to be odd behavior. . .reading email, while on a break from running for your life. The in-box folder opened to reveal his new mail. There were four of them, but one of the four was of great interest. It was from John.

No! Zach didn't want to believe it. He opened the electronic letter, and all suspicions were instantly confirmed. It wasn't going to be necessary to go out on the web and try to trace the account. Instead, he was looking at all the proof he could've ever asked for. The letter read as follows:

Zach,
I wish it hadn't come to this, son. Why didn't you just leave it alone? Now everything has become very complicated. I think we need to discuss some things, don't you? Please come by the office today. I'll be expecting you. And, by the way, Taylor Williams has decided to become my guest until we've concluded this negotiation.
John.

Zach screamed with fury. "That bastard's got her. He's got the woman I love." But it all made sense. John knew the projects, and he knew the methods. And all expenses came to him, so he was in a position to authorize payment of suspect telephone charges, that is, if they weren't being taken care of by the system. Who would question it? It's not up to an accounts payable clerk to question. What did they know or even care for that matter?

It was all really quite brilliant. The only problem was that it was out and out stealing. Nothing was new about it. It was all stuff that had been tried before. Some people got away with it, some didn't. The only interesting twist about this was that the software house itself, which knew everything about the system, was the responsible party. No computer hacker was to blame this time or faulty program. Zach wondered who besides John was involved. Maybe Bob? Maybe someone else in upper management. All indications were that there had to be several people, at least two. It would take at least management, plus an excellent techie, to do the actual coding. Zachery's mind wondered back to the events of earlier, specifically the guards at his office. The lynchmen who came after Zach didn't have anything to do with the actual crime he figured, they were just hired help. They just took orders and didn't ask questions.

It would be a miracle for someone to catch it, sheer chance. Zach wouldn't even have caught it if it hadn't have been for a simple accident. He fell asleep and ended up at the office late one night on a particular night when no one should have been there.

The events played over and over, exactly the same, all night long. Finally the dim light of dawn broke the daze that Zachery had been in. *'It would be 8:00 soon, business hours,'* he thought, as he chanced a short peek out the window. He realized they were probably watching his apartment, so he couldn't go there. It wouldn't be safe, no matter what John said.

Once again they had the upper hand. Their ace in the hole was the woman Zachery loved. They knew he would play the game by their rules now, which meant no police and no press.

All he could think about was Taylor. He could lose his career. He could lose his money. He could lose his self respect. But he couldn't lose Taylor Williams. She was the one thing he couldn't bear to lose.

Chapter
Nineteen

Zachery's car sat idling by the street side a small distance from the compound as he leaned on the hood. He was watching. This was almost the same spot he had used last night to survey the compound before entering. He had thought it over time and again and knew that there was no way to avoid the meeting with John.

With a deep breath, he got back in his car and drove to the front entrance where a guard slowed him down, saw who he was and waved him on grudgingly. The car rolled to a stop in front of the building. His eyes scanned the entire complex. It was the building where he'd worked and been happy for so many years. A chill ran through him as a gust of cold wind whipped across the parking lot. Staring at the sixth floor windows, he wondered if it was the wind or windows that had sent the chill through his weary body. Dark storm clouds rolled over the building. A drizzle had begun to fall as Zach pulled his jacket closed and started toward the Global office building. The weather sure did match the task at hand, though. What a great day for a little kidnapping, espionage and treason. Zach hoped it wouldn't also be a day for bloodshed.

How could this have been going on for so long? He felt betrayed. How come he hadn't noticed it before? Maybe he wasn't that smart after all. Maybe John had been playing him for a fool all these years while laughing and mocking him behind his back. The confusion was driving him crazy. He felt as though it was all a lie.

Even after all the bad in his life right now, there was still one good thing. . .Taylor. He loved her, she meant the world to him. Whatever it took, he would get her back.

He slowly walked into the building, and his heart sped to a rapid pace yet again. As he walked through the downstairs lobby towards the elevator, he noticed something. The lobby was full of people, as usual. There were people around him, but everyone was avoiding him. Several women off to one side whispered to each other and kept peeking around at him. What was this? Zachery stopped and looked around slowly. He almost panicked and ran back out, but got a grip on himself and started walking again. He ran into a friend by the elevator. They entered the elevator, but the other man stared down at his feet without saying a word.

"What's going on here, Frank?" he asked the man, referring to the incident in the lobby. Frank looked up at him for just a moment and then quickly looked back down at the floor.

He shrugged his shoulders and said, "I don't know, what do you mean?"

"Oh, c'mon, Frank." Zachery said raising his voice, "I've been here five minutes, and everyone's treating me like I have AIDS or leprosy or something." They looked each other in the eye for a long time. "Well, c'mon," Zachery added, hoping to pry something out of him.

"You really don't know, do you?" Frank asked, dismayed.

"Know what?" Zachery raised his voice.

"Well, Zachery," he started in a low voice. "There's a rumor going around that you've been sabotaging programs and stealing money. Everybody thinks that you're one of these computer pirates, right here in our own company."

The elevator stopped, and the door opened. Zachery was shocked.

"Zachery, I don't know if this is true or not." The man had a burst of courage when the elevator opened providing him with an exit. "But, if it is, I hope they send you to prison for a long, long time. Everyone here believed in you and trusted in you." With that Frank left the elevator at a jog.

Zachery leaned out and yelled after him, "I'm innocent. It's not me doing it, it's them."

Frank ignored him as he turned down a hallway and out of sight.

Zachery jumped back in the elevator as the door was closing, to continue towards his meeting with John.

"Damn they're good." Zachery whispered. His voice trailed off, while the thought continued. *'They leaked those stories about me into the grapevine. Now I'm the bad guy and the whole company's on their side. They're in the clear and I'm the one on the defensive.'*

A guard opened the door leading into the computer room, and Zach went through. The guard stared intently at him. He had obviously been instructed to let him through. Work stopped as everybody watched the spectacle that was Zach Crawford. He walked across the computer room in total silence. They sure didn't try to hide their curiosity, just stopping everything to stare at the crook, the freak.

Zach stepped through the door exiting the computer room, leading into the hallway of his and John's offices. *'That was a short stay,'* he pondered about his new office. It was a slight relief to get out of sight of everyone, but Zach continued on walking down the plush hall that he'd been so familiar with. John's secretary looked up from her desk and immediately tried to call John to warn him. She was too late.

Zachery swung the door open hard, letting it hit the wall and stepped in. The crash surprised John, who had been looking at the morning paper. He sure was calm and collected, though. He obviously felt he was in control. The paper rustled loudly as John folded it together and tossed it to a corner of his desk. The secretary came stumbling in to defend herself.

"I'm sorry, sir. He just barged right in without saying anything."

John slowly rose from his seat, putting his hands in his pockets. "That's alright. Leave us alone."

"Yes, sir," she answered with intimidation.

"Close the door on your way out," he added as she walked away.

With the door closed, they stood motionless, staring at each other for a very long time. Each tried to read the other's thoughts, find his weaknesses. . .anything to gain the upper hand.

"Well, well," John said finally.

Zachery remained still.

"Zachery, why did you have to do this?"

"Where's Taylor?" Zachery asked, ignoring John's question.

"Don't worry about her," John snapped. "We'll get to that in a minute."

Zach's hands began to quiver slightly as his nervousness and anger grew stronger.

"Tell me why, Zach," John asked again.

"Are you kidding? You want to know why?" Zach exploded. "The reason why is that I worked my ass off for this company. I believed in it. Then one day I stumble into someone stealing from the company, but no one cares. I wanted to help my company, but no one was interested. But hell, you know why that is? Because the company itself is the fucking thief!"

"Oh, come on, Zach," John yelled back at him. "We're not playing house here. We're here for the same reason everyone else is. . .to do whatever it takes to make money. Besides, that money you're talking about is pennies and nickels and dimes. Nobody even misses it."

"That little bit adds up to a lot, and even if it were just a little, it's still stealing."

"Let's forget all this, my boy." John toned down his voice, to try and reason with Zach. "We can make millions together. Everyone agrees to your joining us. You'd be a great asset. With your expertise we could double our money."

"Who else is involved? I know it's more than you. You might as well tell me."

"Zach," John chuckled. "You have no idea."

"I have some ideas, all right. And when I go to the police, we'll see if I'm right."

"You don't have a clue, son." John mocked him. "But you know what? I might as well tell ya. Because, you're not going anywhere. Remember our little blonde secret?"

"Who is it?" Zach demanded.

"Who do you think?" John paused, only for effect. "VonEric and Little."

Zach was amazed that John was so free with the names. It worried him. Why would they give him this much information unless they weren't particularly worried about him spilling his guts later.

VonEric and Little, Zach considered. Neither was a surprise. Zach had always been uneasy about working for VonEric, always questioned the man's integrity. VonEric was a money hungry, power hungry crook, just as he'd always suspected. Little was a different story, though. It made sense. He was getting up there in age, not old, but definitely not going anywhere in his career. A real slob of a man, Little had gone for the money, plain and simple.

"So. . .Are you with us, Zach?" John returned to his calm sincere approach once again.

"Are you joking?" Zach smirked. "I wouldn't join you people. You make me sick to my stomach."

John's fury flared. "Get off your goddamn high and mighty pedestal. It's not like you're free of sin." He was screaming at the top of his voice.

Zach was puzzled and didn't answer him.

John watched his reaction, then began laughing. After a long pause he laughed and said, "Yeah, we know about the phone calls you've been getting from college buddy. Let's see, what's his name. . .oh yeah, Curry."

"Just what do you know?" Zach stuttered, beginning to panic.

"We know all about initiation night, about the hazing."

"What do you know? How do you know?" Zach asked, emphasizing his question in disbelief.

"Well, my boy," John started, believing that he was now in complete control of the situation. "If you're a top programmer in this company, what's your business is our business. And what you say, we hear. What you hear, we. . . hear. . .too."

"Are you saying that my house is bugged?"

There was no answer.

"For how long?"

Still no answer.

"You sons of bitches!"

John slowly walked over to Zach and placed his open hands out. "Give me the disk," he ordered Zach as though disgusted that this lowlife was wasting his time.

"I want Taylor first."

John frowned. "You know, I could have a couple guards come in here and take it from you. Then I could have them haul you out of here and the company would press charges against YOU for embezzlement."

"I may be a little naive, John. But, I'm not stupid enough to walk in this place with that disk in my hip pocket."

"All right, Zach, you wanna play games? Well, I'm good at playing games." John smiled ever so slightly. It was the expression of a man accustomed to getting his way. He walked around to the back side of his desk and sat down in the leather chair. His large hands reached across the desk and starting wrestling with the newspaper.

Zachery knew he was up to something as he watched the pages turning.

Finally he looked up at Zach, smiling again, then took his fingertips and spun around the paper, bringing an article to Zach's attention.

The story was about a young man who had been found dead along the lakeshore. The man had been beaten severely, then shot three times in the chest. IT WAS CURRY, the man who was blackmailing Zach.

The color drained from Zach's face. His eyes were blank, and a lump stuck in his throat. He couldn't say anything at all.

"We had a long talk with your friend. He was reluctant at first, but he finally decided to tell us the whole story. So Zach, as you can see, we took care of your problem. Now I think you can help us take care of ours."

"I had nothing to do with this, John, and you know it."

"Oh, but that's not the impression I get," John smirked. "According to the report, the gun used in the murder was a .38 caliber." He paused. "Don't YOU have a .38?" Zach couldn't speak. He was terrified. Surely they didn't steal the gun from his nightstand. Finally he managed to say, "Yeah, so?"

"SO?" John yelled. "It was your gun, you idiot!" John's face turned blank. "You give us the disk, Zach, or we'll use the other three bullets on your pretty blonde girlfriend. Then we'll turn the gun in to the police. . .say you had been acting strangely and went off the deep end. I have this feeling that when two upstanding citizens of this community, such as myself and Mr. VonEric go to the DA's office, they'll believe just about anything."

John smiled at him before continuing. "For instance, you came to us a week ago. You were on the verge of a breakdown and told us both that Curry was blackmailing you, and Taylor was his girlfriend. She was working on the inside. She knew you were stealing from Global, a company that took you in off the street and made you who you are today. So you shot them. You shot them both to protect yourself from being found out."

Zach stepped back a step as though pushed off balance. He was unable to comprehend this devious scheme. The skies had darkened even further. In the distance, lightning bolted across the sky. He watched as John played out the part, rain now pelting the window behind him, providing his macabre backdrop.

"Well, Mr. District Attorney, we tried to get him some help. I guess it was just too late. We found this gun in his desk and knew that we should contact the police right away."

Zach was silent, searching for an escape from this plan. "What about the disk? I can show it to them."

"Zach, they would convict you of murdering Miss Williams, this character in the paper, and possibly the poor guy in your fraternity. After all that, do you think they'd believe your story? That would just be another charge to tack on. Do you want to add embezzlement to the charges against you. You'd be lucky to just get a life sentence over the electric chair."

"Okay, okay!" Zach said in submission. "If I give it to you, will Taylor go unharmed?"

"Yes Zach, I give you my word. Just give us that disk and the two of you can walk away from this place forever."

Zachery sighed heavily, feeling beaten. He didn't believe for a minute that Taylor was safe. They were probably both dead after John got the disk.

"Where and when do you want it?"

"Do you know where our storage facility is, just north of town?"

Zachery shook his head. "I'll be there with the disk at midnight tonight."

"I'll be there with the girl, and we can make the switch. There shouldn't be anyone there that late. And come alone, Zachery."

Zach glared into John's eyes. How could he have been so wrong about him? He wasn't a good man at all. He was a cold-hearted son of a bitch. Zach had trusted him for so many years, and now just the sight of John sickened him. He wheeled around to leave. As he placed his hand on the doorknob, he turned back to John.

"I'll be there."

Chapter Twenty

"What'll it be, pal?"

Zach looked across the bar to the voice of the bartender.

"What'll you have?" he said again impatiently.

It was 10:00. Zach had come here hoping a drink would calm him down. His stomach was turning circles, feeling queasy and shaky ever since the meeting with John. It'd been the longest day of his life. He wondered if he was too nervous to go through with the meeting. Couldn't he just run? No. There was no alternative, but to go through with it. Taylor needed him. She was depending on him.

His hands shook violently as he reached for the double shot of whiskey just returned by the bartender. He downed it in one drink and tried to shake off the chill it sent through his body. He ordered another and also drank it in one drink. The liquor burned his empty stomach and churned around for several minutes.

He glanced around the bar room. A neon "Old Style " sign lit the tiny place from the back wall. It was nearly deserted, except for two uniformed men who were shooting pool on an undersized table in desperate need of new cloth. It was obvious why the felt wasn't replaced after one of the men, so drunk he could barely stand, fell against the table and spilled most of his beer across it.

"Hey, Stan," the bartender yelled. "Hey, Stan! Your old lady's on the phone."

The other of the two men slowly turned to face the bar. Zach could see now that according to the uniforms, they were utility workers. And this must be Stan, judging from the name stitched to the left chest pocket.

"What does she want?" he demanded belligerently.

"How the hell do I know?" the bartender snapped back. "Maybe she wants to smoke my pipe."

Stan glared at the bartender for just a moment, then snickered at the remark instead while he snatched the phone from his hand.

"What do you want?" he said, no less hostile.

A short pause.

"I'll get the damn formula," he preached into the receiver. "I told you that this morning. Why da ya have to keep calling me down here for? All you wanna do is bitch. I don't know why. . ."

Zach turned away from Stan and noticed an older lady sitting at the far end of the bar worshipping what must have been her seventh or eighth rum and coke. Zach felt sorry for her. She looked lonely. He wondered if she had never allowed herself to love a man or maybe just hadn't ever found the right man. Or he might be assuming too much, that she even wanted to find someone. Her clothing looked nice enough, like someone he would expect to see in the office. Had she worked her whole life away only for this? Was this existence her reward? Stopping at this bar every evening after working until 7:00 or 8:00, guzzling the rest of the evening away before stumbling home to bed and being certain to set that alarm so that the ritual could go on again the next day. . .

'I can't let this happen to me,' he thought to himself as he stared into the empty shot glass. 'I've already wasted too

much of my life. Taylor has shown me what I've been missing. I never realized just how empty my life was.'
The loneliness almost becomes your friend. . .your only friend. You get so used to it, that it dulls your senses. It becomes routine and you stop realizing you're alone. *'I've pushed people out of my life since I was. . .since that night in college. Have I paid my dues? Can I let myself be happy now? I love her. . .more than life itself.'*
Zach took a couple of deep breaths then looked at his watch. It was time to go: 11:00. He had no idea what to expect, only that it wouldn't be as simple as he and John just making the trade.
The drive seemed forever, with cornfields lining both sides of the desolate highway. In the darkness thousands of bright stars lit his way, the only lights for miles other than his headlights. It was very dark. The rain from earlier had cleared, and the sky was completely free of clouds.
Suddenly Zach spotted a pair of headlights swinging out behind him on what had previously been a deserted road. He panicked and pushed the accelerator to the floor, trying to lose them. He quickly realized that there was no point in it. The car kept its distance, about a half of a mile behind him, but didn't let him get away either.
Finally Zach saw a small group of lights on the right and up the road a little bit. That was it. He began slowing down and turned down the dirt road which led to the building. The car that had been following him turned also, but still kept a safe distance. Turning his attention forward again, Zach noticed the gates. The white chain link fencing was already unlocked and swung open. *'The gates of Hell,'* he thought.
Zachery slowed his car to a crawl, trying to be very careful to avoid any sort of ambush. He stopped and surveyed the grounds before continuing. They seemed deserted. The building was a large, metal warehouse type structure. It stood several stories tall and covered about as much area as a football field. The paint was a dirty white color, and the sides had the company logo across it, painted in bright green.
Zachery finally inched his car to a stop about fifty yards from a single open door with a light shining down. The car behind him had also stopped now, just inside the gate, still maintaining its distance. Whoever it was didn't seem in-

terested in coming closer for now. The driver stayed inside the car. With a closer look, Zach thought he recognized it as one of the cars that had shown up when he was breaking into his office building.

He walked towards the door where he assumed they were hiding. With each step he could hear the dirt compacting louder under his feet. The adrenaline filled his veins as it had many times during this whole ordeal. His heart thumped loudly, and he felt so weak that he was worried about his knees buckling. But they didn't, each step drawing him closer to the open door until finally he stood in the doorway.

He didn't see anyone, but they were there. He could feel it. Metal shelves, 30 feet tall, filled the building. This was a storage facility that Global used for old equipment and office supplies such as paper, cleaners and furniture. Many shelves were empty, while occasional groups had dusty boxes stacked several rows high.

Zach walked through the empty aisles towards the center of the building, where the only light source was emanating from. At the end of the aisle a large space opened up in the center of the building. It seemed that the overhead lighting in this area was the only light turned on in the whole building.

Mustering up his courage, Zach turned and stepped from the row and then gasped in shock. It was Taylor. She was tied to a chair sitting in the middle of the opening, and three men stood behind her, indistinguishable so far, due to the combination of poor lighting and the distance between them.

Zach Crawford took a few steps toward them before he was told to stop. He did, but was close enough now to see who they were. It was the ringleaders, as he suspected. First John, then VonEric, and last of all the programmer, Dave Little. Zach never knew Little that well, but he could see the balding head, rough face and that disgusting huge pot belly. It was him all right.

It looked like an Old West showdown. Zachery stood absolutely still, his eyes darting between Taylor and the three men behind her while they all stared blankly back at him. A sixth sense told him that the man who'd followed him in the car was now standing behind him. He didn't turn his head, however, deciding not to acknowledge it.

After what seemed an eternity, John finally made the first move. "Where's the disk, Zachery?" he said, walking forward until he was beside Taylor.

"It's inside my jacket pocket. Here." Zachery said motioning inside his right breast pocket. "First untie Taylor, though."

John frowned, "You're not in any position to be bargaining."

Zachery knew he was right. He reached slowly into his pocket, pulled the disk out and gently placed it on the floor. With a quick tap, he pushed it about ten feet in front of him.

Little ran forward and grabbed the disk, whisking it off to a terminal behind him.

"Now. Give me Taylor!" Zachery demanded.

"Just a minute, Zach. We have to make sure that it's the real disk."

It scared him. They had no intention of letting them go, and this stall proved it.

A minute later, the programmer turned to them saying, "It's real. This is it."

Immediately VonEric started laughing, almost a hysterical cackle. Zachery could see that he was a ruthless madman, and now he was sure of what he had been afraid to admit earlier. He and Taylor were to be killed, as simple as that.

"Kill them," VonEric commanded, with as much ease as ordering coffee from his secretary.

VonEric turned his attention to the records which the programmer was going through, and John pulled a gun from a shoulder holster hidden under his suit jacket. It was Zachery's. The same old gun that he had been afraid to touch for so many years since killing the pledge that night, and the same gun that had killed his blackmailer, was now the gun intended to end his life.

"You see, Zach," John began. "We just can't let you go. With a little bit of imagination, the police can put a nice story together. They'll find you and Taylor, both dead, with this gun and your suicide confession note with you, all in your apartment."

"What note?" Zachery asked airily.

"Well, you caught Taylor and your blackmailer friend Curry having an affair, killed them both with your gun and then couldn't live with yourself so you turned the gun on yourself. There's even a few things in your desk to help the police along."

"John," Zachery said and then paused a moment. "I can't believe you would do this." It was one last desperate appeal.

"I'm sorry, son," he answered coldly. "I don't have any choice."

John raised the gun from his side and pointed it directly at Zach, who was motionless, in shock. Suddenly Taylor kicked at John's arm from down in her seat. Just as he fired, his arm was knocked sideways, causing him to miss. Zach felt paralyzed, he couldn't move, couldn't do anything. In a blind rage, John swung his arm and jabbed the gun to Taylor's ear.

"Get her later," VonEric screamed in a deep voice. "He's gonna get away."

Zachery regained his senses as he heard the other gunman coming up behind him. Then he saw John swing his arm back up to take aim again. He dove into an aisle, just as John was firing. The bullet sped by, missing him and hitting the gunman who was just behind him instead. Blood sprayed all around him. The man's body hit the hard concrete floor beside Zach with a thud. It jerked about with muscle spasms for only a moment before the man was completely dead.

Zach was kneeling in the aisle, staring at the dead man whose cold lifeless eyes were still open, staring back at him. Then he noticed the gun the man was holding. He had to get it. It might be their only chance. Looking back at John, there was no time to waste. John would chase him down without giving a thought to the man that he had just accidentally killed.

Drawing a deep breath, he reached his arm out into the opening and grabbed the barrel of the gun. It was covered with blood. The man's grip was still firm, and the gun had to be yanked from his hand. Zachery felt sick, like he needed to vomit, but there was no time for that. The body and blood were still warm, even though the life was gone and the man was dead. He took several more deep breaths to calm his churning stomach. He was terrified as he realized that John had hesitated long enough for him to get the gun.

John was aggravated at himself for missing and shooting one of his own men but quickly deduced that Zach now had a gun also, and he was in danger. He took cover, off to the opposite side of the big opening.

Zach looked at the gun he now held in his hand. It was a terrible reminder of that night so long ago when he was in college. He hadn't fired a gun since that night and started trembling at the thought. But he knew that he had to overcome his fear. Taylor needed him.

Leaning his head out from the aisle just a bit, he surveyed the area. After moving out far enough, he could see John trying to hide behind a large box, frantically turning to and fro in search of him. At that instant he was spotted, and John reeled off two quick shots. Zach pulled himself back in, and the shots went astray, one of them striking and denting the metal shelf behind him. He leaned out again. John was still behind the box, but something else was terribly wrong.

VonEric had attacked Taylor, who was still helplessly bound. The chair was hanging sideways and VonEric's grip was tight around Taylor's neck. He watched as VonEric reached into his pocket with one hand and pulled a knife from it. The blade swung open freely. Zachery knew that this was the time to act. It had to be now. He raised his gun and aimed it straight at VonEric. As he looked down the barrel, his whole arm began to shake, and that night flashed back into his head. The gun shook so violently that there was no way that Zach could even come close to hitting VonEric.

"Zachery," he heard in a whisper. "Zachery!" He snapped out of it. Taylor was screaming for his help. His arm steadied as he lined up again. The sights blurred slightly and Zach refocused on VonEric.

"VonEric," he screamed.

Startled, VonEric released his grip on Taylor, letting her fall to the floor, gasping for air. In his arrogance, VonEric turned towards Zach and started walking slowly towards him. Hatred gleamed in his eyes.

Zach was ready, though. He pulled the hammer back on the gun as VonEric came closer. Suddenly VonEric realized that his adversary wasn't bluffing. He stopped in his tracks with the hateful eyes still gleaming. There was no turning back now. Zach had been pushed to the limit. Before he could change his mind, he squeezed the trigger and watched VonEric crumble to the floor. Zach looked at the lifeless body across from him. There was no remorse.

Sensing an opportunity, John rose from behind the box and fired his gun again and again. He kept squeezing the trigger, but nothing was coming out. It was empty. Zach didn't care about John, though. He was watching Taylor, who lay on the floor, bound to the chair.

"Taylor!" Zach screamed frantically.

"I'm okay, Zach," she answered, trying to catch her breath. "Get out of here. Save yourself."

"No. Hold on, I'm coming."

Suddenly, Zachery noticed Dave Little, directly behind where Taylor lay on the floor. He'd put the disk into his briefcase and was trying to run away. Zach quickly fired his gun again, the shots flying straight over Taylor. At this distance, however, he missed the pot-bellied programmer.

Desperate, he fired a third time, but this bullet struck a gas tank on the back of a forklift in the background, igniting it into a huge ball of flames. The blast blew the man to the ground and covered him with fuel, while the flames roared off the fork truck, onto the gas soaked floor, and right up the programmer's body.

Little screamed in agony as he ran in circles, desperately trying to find help. And he did, running towards John while the flames on his back grew larger. John had reloaded his gun and turned it on his partner when he saw him coming. He shot twice before halting Little's advance.

The flames spread rapidly as the fuel found its way to some cleaning chemicals in one of the aisles. A huge explosion resulted with a small mushroom cloud of fire billowing to the ceiling. The whole area became engulfed in flames in only a few moments.

Zach began scooting his way along the floor towards Taylor. But John reappeared from a different spot with his reloaded gun. He fired twice at Zach, who violently rolled to the side to avoid being hit. He lay still for a moment. The flames were growing, the building hazy, as smoke continued to fill it. He had to get to Taylor soon.

A faint noise caught his ears. It was her, coughing for air. She lay helpless on the floor, tied to the chair still. He had to help her. If he could only get to her. . .. Then he heard a horrified scream. He jumped up thinking that it was too late, that the flames had reached her. But that wasn't it. Taylor's eyes were turned to John, who was standing in a far aisle laughing, with his gun pointing at her this time. Zach could barely see him through all the hot smoke. The building was getting very hot as more and more flamed up around them.

The dirty sweat poured from John's face as he squinted to aim at her.

"No!" yelled Zachery frantically.

In one motion he swung his gun up and fired one more time at John, who had ignored his scream. The desperate shot was on the mark, miraculously. The bullet pierced the skin on the left side of John's neck, exiting through the other side. His body spun a complete circle and jerked in violent convulsions as blood spewed from the hole in his neck with each pulse of his heart. It looked as though he needed to scream with the pain, but the bullet had mangled his throat to where he couldn't even draw a breath of the smoke–filled air into his lungs. He stumbled back several steps before spinning and falling face first into a box and sliding to the concrete floor. That was all of them.

Zachery jumped to his feet and ran to Taylor, who was still lying in the floor, tied to the chair. He slid to a stop in front of her and immediately untied the knots that bound her.

"Oh God. Are you okay?" he asked in a shaky voice. "Please forgive me, Taylor. . .Oh God."

Taylor shook her head and nervously said yes. He got the ropes loose enough for her to pull free and rapidly helped her to her feet. They embraced, tighter than ever before.

"Zach," she said, looking into his eyes with tears streaming down her cheeks. "I knew you'd come. I knew it. I love you."

He pulled her tight to him again and whispered, "I love you, too."

Suddenly he pulled away, realizing that they weren't yet out of danger. The flames had grown all around them, creating a wall of fire.

"We've got to get out of here," he yelled over top of the burning sounds of the building.

Chapter
Twenty-one

Taylor looked back through the blaze at the programmer's scorched body, lying close to the mangled forklift. It was disgusting how the fire burned him. Then Zach started pulling her towards the exit and away from the body.

"Zach, wait," she yelled, turning to him. "Get his briefcase."

"Why?" he asked frantically.

"That's the proof we need," she replied. "They put all the files on what they were doing in that briefcase before you got here. They had them stored in a safe somewhere in this building. And Zach, whatever they had on you is in there, too."

"Okay, wait here," he yelled. The building was filled with smoke and burnt lumber, and supplies began falling around them from everywhere. Zach weaved and jumped obstacles which were falling in his path as he tried to reach the man less than 20 yards away. His breaths were short as he coughed for air while his lungs were filling with smoke. The smoke was so thick that Zach had to stop and search for the body again after rubbing his burning, watery eyes. He took several more steps and knelt down, grasping the briefcase. The intense heat of the fire had almost melted the dark leather. He yanked it up and turned back towards Taylor, whom he could barely see through the thick, black smoke.

"Taylor," he yelled.

"Over here, I'm okay."

He spotted her again. She was still where he'd left her.

Zachery looked down at the case again and started thinking. *'This case is all I need. It has all the records, how much money they've taken and who it was taken from. And it would prove my innocence.'*

'But what about the secret? If I'm right, everyone that knew about it is lying dead in this room. It's terrible, but I almost believe that my secret is safe again. Just living with this terrible secret should be enough punishment, shouldn't it? I'll never forgive myself, and I'm sure that I'll always be haunted by the nightmare.'

'But maybe Taylor could help me. With her love and compassion, this thing might be put behind me. I love her more than anything. She's the best thing to ever happen to me. All the status, power and money in the world don't mean anything without love, without her. I realize that now. I've wasted so much of my life striving for all the wrong goals, but not anymore. I want to grow old with this woman. . . have that loving face to come home to every day, lie down her with every evening, and wake up beside her every morning. That's what's important.'

He looked up from the case. His face was burning from the flames around him, and sweat dripped into his dry burning eyes as he made his way across the rubble–filled floor. John lay face down in front of Zach. He looked at the body with regret. It's too bad it had to end like this. But this wasn't the man Zach had grown to love as a father. How could he have been so wrong?

Zach's eyes turned away, but then caught a glimpse of something else. The .38 caliber revolver was still in John's hand. This gun had done enough killing. He considered picking it up, but couldn't stomach the thought of holding it in his hand again. Hopefully this .38 caliber has seen its last action. Let it lie. It seemed right that it perish here in this damned inferno.

Suddenly, a loud noise broke him from his thoughts. It was a deep creaking noise from above them, drowning out the crackling sounds of the burning supplies. He looked up, seemingly in slow motion, afraid of what he would see. There was a large wooden platform, charred heavily and swaying on its now weak supports.

"No, this can't be happening," he whispered aloud. The platform was directly over Taylor.

"Taylor, look out," he screamed as loud as he could. But it was too late.

With the loud crack of a support board breaking in half, the platform gave way. Zach was still too far away. All he could do was watch the boards come down on top of her, and a deadly scream followed.

The large, thick planks viciously knocked her to the floor and pinned her there in agony. Some of the splintered wood lay across her stomach and covered both legs, portions of it still smoldering only inches from her fragile body. Taylor's face cringed as she screamed in agony from a broken rib.

Zachery was in disbelief. His heart raced uncontrollably as he knelt beside her. How could this be happening? Was he to be punished even more?

"Oh my God, Taylor," he said, as the tears formed in his eyes. "Just sit tight, I'll get these off of you. Oh God, what have I done?"

"Help me, Zach, please," she pleaded with him between her screams.

Zach was doing the best he could, though already in a total state of panic. He looked at the boards lying across her and placed his hands on one. He immediately jerked back as it scorched his hands. *'Oh God. In another minute it'll be burning her, too.'* He swung around several times in a circle looking for something, anything, to use to move the boards.

He looked back down at the boards and at Taylor's pain–filled face. The beauty was masked. He had to get the boards off of her. Another idea popped into his head.

Quickly Zach ripped his shirt up and wrapped his hands with it so that they would be somewhat protected from the burns. Reaching down with wrapped hands, he grabbed the board and pulled again, grunting with every ounce of energy he could summon. It still wouldn't move.

"Hurry Zach," she pleaded. "It's starting to burn through."

Then he saw a long metal pipe a few feet away and grabbed it with his throbbing hands. He slammed it under the board, and with a final groan of effort, Zach pried the board up ever so little.

"Taylor, scoot out from under it," Zach yelled, holding his breath as he tried to hold it.

She used her legs to scoot out from under the boards. As soon as she was clear, Zach released the pipe, exhausted. It crashed to the floor loudly. All Zach could think about was Taylor's welfare. He knelt beside her, lifting her head into the palm of his hands.

"You're gonna be okay," he said trembling.

She opened her eyes and looked at him. Her pain was obvious, but she would be okay.

Zach gently helped Taylor to her feet. She winced in pain from the rib, but seemed okay otherwise.

"Stop right there!" a voice called from a dark aisle.

It was a voice Zach recognized well, with a certain odd drawl that he'd become so accustomed to. 'This can't be happening,' he told himself. 'We won, we beat them. We had all the evidence and we were out of danger. Why, God, why?'

"Bob?" Zach questioned, as he and Taylor turned toward the voice. "Not you, too, Bob?"

Bob stepped from the darkness, a large shotgun pointed in their direction. He moved slowly and with confidence, seemingly very accustomed to handling firearms.

Zach stared at his friend in disbelief. How could this be happening? He watched as Bob shouldered the shotgun in one smooth motion.

A blast of fire exploded from the barrel. The shot was deafening. Zach gripped Taylor's hand tightly, preparing to die. His only thought was of her soft hand in his.

But nothing happened. They weren't dead. They weren't hit! Zach looked at his friend with confusion, then realized the truth. Spinning around, Zach and Taylor caught a final glimpse of VonEric. His entire chest spewed blood onto a white dress shirt and the business suit. The buckshot from Bob's weapon had crushed his chest, finishing him for good this time. The lifeless body toppled backward, blown back from the force. Zach knew that he wouldn't be getting up again, not this time.

"No buddy. Not me, too!" Bob's voice carried disappointment that his friend would even consider such a possibility. "And next time, you could try moving out of the way."

"But. . .How did you know? How did you find us?" Zach was totally dumbfounded.

"I been followin' ya since your meeting with John this morning." Bob's tone was back to normal. "I didn't know what was up, but I knew you weren't doing any embezzling. I figured you was bein' set up. So I followed ya. You picked up a tail right after you left that bar, so I dropped back and followed him instead. And this is where it led me. I'm sorry I wasn't here sooner, but when I was sneakin' around outside, the shootin' started. I had to run back and get my friend here." Bob patted the Winchester pump shotgun as you normally would a trusted pet.

Another walkway crumbled closeby, throwing a mushroom cloud of smoke their way. It brought them back to reality.

"Let's go!" Zach yelled. "We gotta get out of here!"

Bob led the way through the darkness and out the door. They ran across the parking lot to the car and turned to see the building in shambles. Taylor's breath was short as she favored her side still.

Flames leapt out the top and smoke billowed from every open crevice. It was dying. The building would crumble within minutes.

"Zach," Bob said. "We should go. The fire department's gonna be here any minute. . .not to mention the cops. What're we gonna tell them?"

"I don't know," Zach answered.

"I think we should take off," Bob reiterated.

"I've been that route, Bob. I was in trouble once and ran away. I don't know if it's the right thing to do." Of course, he referred to the memory of the pledge and the terrible incident with Curry.

"Zach. I'm telling you this as your friend. Let it go. This thing is over. You did what you had to do here, but the cops might not understand that! Let's go."

"Zach, honey." Taylor touched her lover's soot covered face. "Bob's right. It'll be okay. There's nothing to feel guilty about. We have to go. . .while we still can."

Zach thought for just a moment. "I know. Go ahead and get in the car. I need to speak to Bob."

Zach turned back to his friend, searching for the words.

"You saved our lives back there, Bob. And you don't even know what this is about."

"Stop right there, pal." Bob waved his hands. "I know you. I don't have to know what this is about. That's your business, not mine. I know you're a good person, and that's what this is about for me."

Zach embraced him, touched by his words.

"I can't stay here," Zach added sadly. "Too many memories, too much bad. I need to start over somewhere else."

"Yeah, I understand."

A small explosion rumbled from somewhere deep inside the warehouse. Toward the back, a section was unable to handle the punishment and caved to the ground. More smoke rolled out and the flames lit the parking lot.

"Bob," started Zach, and he offered the briefcase to his friend. "This has all the information; everything's here."

Bob opened the case and glanced at the files inside. One folder contained the label "Zach Crawford." He handed it back to Zach and closed the lid. Then with a mighty heave, Bob slung the briefcase across the lot where it landed beside one of the cars. There it would be found in the ensuing investigation. . .

"That's that!" Bob commanded. "You've got your file and the police have theirs."

"Thanks, Bob," Zach whispered. He was as sincere as he'd ever been at any time in his life.

"You get goin' now, Zach." Even Bob seemed on the verge of an emotional outburst. "Take care of yourself. . . And if you ever need a friend, I'm here."

Zach climbed into the car and watched as Bob lumbered towards his old Caddy. Not once did he turn back to them, only a quick wave as he sped past.

"Well," Zach sighed. "Where to?"

They both shared a chuckle at the expense of Taylor's aching ribcage. It was such a huge decision to make, but at that moment seemed as trivial as choosing a T-shirt to lounge in.

"How's Florida sound?" he prodded.

"Has a nice ring to it, I think," Taylor answered.

Zach Crawford turned the key, and the engine roared to life. As he spun the car around, he took Taylor's hand into his and turned due south.

If you would like to order a copy or copies of *The LakeShore Project*, please send your name, shipping address, number of copies, $12.95 per copy, plus $3.50 per copy for shipping/handling. Send check or money order to:

Mark D. Vance
P.O. Box 351186
Jacksonville, Fl 32235-1186

Or, if you have any comments, feel free to mail them to the above address, or check out my website - located at http://users.cybermax.net/~mvance. You can also email me at <mvance@cybermax.net>.